Updated Edition

BELIEVE *to* ACHIEVE

SEE THE INVISIBLE, DO THE IMPOSSIBLE

HOWARD "H" WHITE
Foreword by Phil Knight

ATRIA PAPERBACK
New York London Toronto Sydney New Delhi

BEYOND WORDS
Portland, Oregon

ATRIA
PAPERBACK
An Imprint of Simon & Schuster, Inc.
1230 Avenue of the Americas
New York, NY 10020

BEYOND WORDS
1750 S.W. Skyline Blvd., Suite 20
Portland, Oregon 97221-2543
503-531-8700 / 503-531-8773 fax
www.beyondword.com

Managing editor: Lindsay S. Easterbrooks-Brown
Editor: Jenefer Angell
Copyeditor: David Abel
Proofreader: Jade Chan
Design: Devon Smith
Composition: William H. Brunson Typography Services

This Atria Paperback/Beyond Words trade paperback edition June 2018

ATRIA PAPERBACK and colophon are trademarks of Simon & Schuster, Inc.
BEYOND WORDS PUBLISHING is an imprint of Simon & Schuster, Inc., and the Beyond Words logo is a registered trademark of Beyond Words Publishing, Inc.

For more information about special discounts for bulk purchases, please contact Simon & Schuster Special Sales at 1-866-506-1949 or business@simonandschuster.com.

The Simon & Schuster Speakers Bureau can bring authors to your live event. For more information or to book an event, contact the Simon & Schuster Speakers Bureau at 1-866-248-3049 or visit our website at www.simonspeakers.com.

Manufactured in the United States of America

10 9 8 7 6 5 4 3 2 1

Library of Congress Cataloging-in-Publication Data

White, Howard, 1950- author.
Title: Believe to achieve updated edition : see the invisible, do the impossible / Howard "H" White ; foreword by Phil Knight.
Description: New York : Atria Paperback ; Hillsboro, Oregon : Beyond Words, [2018]
Identifiers: LCCN 2018015174 | ISBN 9781582706900 (pbk.) | ISBN 9781439116784 (ebook)
Subjects: LCSH: Success--Psychological aspects.
Classification: LCC BF637.S8 W453 2018 | DDC 158.1--dc23
LC record available at https://lccn.loc.gov/2018015174

The corporate mission of Beyond Words Publishing, Inc.: *Inspire to Integrity*

To Mandy

from Granny
through Dad

You, my Little Bear, complete my circle.

CONTENTS

Contents

ACKNOWLEDGMENTS

In my original 2003 book, *Believe to Achieve*, I acknowledged everyone that had a part in shaping my life. You know who you are and I want to thank you again. You've meant more to me than you will ever know. Thank You!!

In this updated and expanded edition of *Believe to Achieve*, I first want to thank the two people that have grown with me.

My wife Donna, the love of my life for over thirty-five years, took a leap of faith and left everything she knew to follow me to the unknown land of Nike, which we discovered together. Without a leap of faith nothing can ever happen. The fear of letting go was real for us. We grew together and I want to pause for a moment to say thank you for believing in my dream, which became our Dream. Donna endured my demanding and overly positive personality. Donna, thank you for accepting me for who I am. You have been more than awesome! You have been my own personal dream come true!!!

Now, to my dearest Mandy. You've brightened our lives. You've been the most courageous and positive person that I've known. You've fought in the face of every adversity. There is nothing that you've been through that has dimmed your spirit and your light. You've made me the proudest parent on the planet. Seeing you find the possible in the impossible is a rare quality, one that you've found and perfected. Keep it and never stop believing in it. You've grown so much since the first book was written. Thinking of how much you've grown and who you've become simply puts a smile on my face. Will life always be perfect? It will always be what life is and that will be your choice. How you choose to see it will determine how far you go. You've been my track star and you've worked extremely hard. I just want you to remember that the real game is the game of life. Keep smiling when things do not to go your way. Thanks for being the light of our life! As a family we have all grown together. Now you've become my grown up "Bear." You've done well my dear! Thanks for letting me come along for the ride.

Love to both of you, your greatest admirer!

Finally, for this new edition of *Believe to Achieve,* I want to acknowledge everyone who has the courage to take that leap of faith, the courage to follow their dreams, and the courage to believe in someone else's dream and push them beyond their limits. You are the ones that make life worth living and the planet a better place for us all.

From Moms to Coach Hathaway, Nancy Knewstep, Coach Driesell, Doctor Leedy, Phil Knight, and everyone at Nike. The courage to believe in someone other than yourself is a wonderful quality. I truly hope that this new edition of *Believe to Achieve* will continue to give many more the power and courage to believe in someone else's possibility. The courage to find the strength when you close your eyes to let go of your fears, and the courage to believe first in yourself. Only then can you find the strength to help another. Go ahead and take that leap of faith! That power will light the world!

And a very special thank you goes to Michelle Martin and Malcolm Teasdale. Michelle pushed me to update and expand upon the original *Believe to Achieve*. She wouldn't rest until it was complete. She became inspired during her "What it Takes" symposiums, where young people responded to *Believe to Achieve* and she knew that it needed to be updated. She wanted it to be revised so that it could also be used as a tool, so that parents and mentors and teachers could benefit from its many teachings. Once that was decided I knew that there was a person in Detroit that was already using it as a tool. Malcolm was using it in the classroom and having great results. I put the two of them together and we now have this 2018 edition of *Believe to Achieve*. Thanks to the both of you for your enduring efforts and unselfishness to help others see the beauty in their own wings through *Believe to Achieve*.

ix

FOREWORD

I was recently asked to give three words that describe Howard White. I said, for me, I only need one: friend.

He is a friend, but not in the "since schooldays" sense, or "we go out in the evening after work." If business is war without bullets (and I believe it is), then Howard White and I have been in the same foxhole for over thirty-five years.

During that time together we fought countless battles, some lost, more won, but always with many lessons learned. But while Howard has much to pass on from his business experiences, it is misleading to say that is the sum of this book, because Howard White is a unique individual.

Before there was any business experience at all there was a set of values instilled in him by his mother, Lillian. She cleaned houses for a living, but she made absolutely certain her five kids grew up "right." And then came his run as an all-everything basketball player out of Hampton Virginia, who starred at the University of Maryland, only to see two knee operations end any expectations of an NBA career. This was a huge setback to be sure, but one that ultimately made him a stronger and better person.

It is from these and other experiences, plus his very unique perspective that Howard has taken the time to write this book, passing on lessons learned that have at their core that for which everyone searches: wisdom.

—PHIL KNIGHT
CEO, President, and Chairman
Nike, Inc.

PREFACE

When I first started writing the core ideas behind *Believe to Achieve*, over fifteen years ago, it started out as a letter to my daughter Mandy. I simply wanted her to have a blueprint of her dad's life—how he got to where he was. All of these years later I'm extremely proud of her and what she's accomplished. Mandy went on to accomplish some amazing feats on her high school track team. In her senior year Mandy was named the MVP at the Oregon State Track Meet. She set records in the 100- and 200-meter dash. She also ran on the 4X100 meter relay team and competed in the long jump. She went on to attend the University of Oregon and became Oregon's first 100 meter All American. More important, she graduated and is an extremely kind and thoughtful person. She is now running professionally and made the semi finals in the 2016 Olympic trials.

The power of "Belief" played a strong and positive effect in her development and all her success. Mandy didn't get there on her own. Nor did I get to where I am today by myself.

My life started out when my mother brought me home in a yellow taxi, down the dusty road that led to our house. This was an ancient time. It was 1950. Before he passed my brother recalled seeing a cloud of dust around us as Moms stepped out of the taxi with her newborn child in her arms. He knew from that day his little brother would somehow make a difference in the world. I've contemplated this many times now. I've asked myself, Why me? I've done many things that some consider great; others have said I've changed their lives. As I think about it now, I know that it all started with that dusty cab ride home.

I've been fortunate in my life, and I've learned many things. I know that there must always be a master and an apprentice. There must be someone to show the path. People at every turn have helped me see far greater things than I alone could have imagined. I ask myself, who or what is responsible for my so-called success? Who put me on this wonderful path of light? There were plenty of times that I could have gone the opposite way. There are always two opposing forces that we face each day. You have a choice: you can pick the light side or the dark side. But you are the only one who can make that choice. You are the one who must live with the consequences. I am grateful that I had people to help me choose the right way.

Not too long ago, I came to the realization that my mother was my Master. I've had many teachers, but Lillian Mitchell White was my Master. She didn't teach me with a lot of big lessons—just small ones every day: Did I make up my bed each day? Did I do my chores? I watched her as she went about her life. A simple life, but she went about it with great pride and dignity. I watched her in the flower garden. I watched as she would help a neighbor or just give someone a cup of sugar. I saw something in her that I needed: a gentle greatness and soft humility that came from her quiet faith—a faith that would get us through every storm that came our way.

It's because of her that I was able to open up to all of the other teachers and teachings that have come into my life. She's also the reason I've been able to share what I've learned with others. Throughout my life, I've seen what extraordinary potential lies inside ordinary people—you can never tell what someone is capable of just by looking at them. This is particularly true for young people. Since founding Nike's "Believe to Achieve" program, I've traveled all over the country speaking to people of all ages, and I've seen people "on fire with desire" from the excitement of their dreams. What they don't always know is how to make those dreams happen.

I've learned through experience that there is a process to making things happen and that it's quite an easy one—as long as you pay attention to the lessons and opportunities that come into your life. There are a few basic principles at work in this process: All of our journeys take the shape of a circle, and at any point and place there is a lesson that can be learned. At any point in the circle, something puts you where you need to be at that point in time. Furthermore, you have to see how your actions affect your life and those around you. We are all connected. When we change our lives for the better, we also change the world for the better, and vice versa.

As I went around speaking to various groups, I looked for a concept that would convey these principles. That is where the "And-I Warrior" spirit comes from. In its simplest form, "And-I" is "And I." It is the self and its connection to everything else:

And I am always with you
And I am all that I can be
And I am an agent for change
And I am a leader
And I am a warrior

I have found that people everywhere, of all ages, respond to this idea and that many of them recognize their own potential and begin to see a clear path to success. My office is overflowing with letters and cards of thanks written by children, youths, and those who work with them, telling me that their lives have been transformed by these principles—they are my And-I Warriors.

This expanded edition of *Believe to Achieve* is a handbook to help others who desire to live their lives according to their dreams. I originally wrote it as two volumes: The Apprentice and The Master. "The Apprentice" is the introduction to a concrete method of goal setting that can help anyone achieve success in the external world; "The Master" is for the reader who has tested out these methods and is ready to delve more deeply into the ideas behind them. After years of feedback from readers, I've now included a "Parent, Teacher, and Mentor Lesson Guide" on how to effectively utilize this book and the lessons within with kids and adult groups.

My hope is that this book will help you realize where it is that you want to be and help you get there and that you will see and unlock the potential inside yourself and inside others. And I hope you understand that you are never alone.

There is always a master and an apprentice.

Are you ready to know where you're going?

Are you ready to follow the road of the And-I
    Warrior, or will any road do?

You can train your mind, body, and soul in the
    way of the And-I.

The circle is your shield, it is your cloak against
    the world.

It is a sign of completeness.

It is a sign of wholeness.

There is no beginning and there is no end.

Go forth my warrior and change the world.

This is your handbook and guide. This is your
passport to the world of the And-I. Your shield is the
circle; your weapon is your mind. Change the world!
Follow me or lead me, but change the world you must.

THE MIRROR BY HOWARD "H" WHITE

This morning I looked in the mirror and didn't
   see me,
I saw an old basketball hoop where I should be.
It was weathered and old, and rusted away,
But, I still remember when it called me to play.
Whether the day was cold or bright sunshine
It really didn't matter because I had to put in
   the time.

It spoke to me in ways I couldn't understand,
But truthfully taught me how to be a man....
I know, I know...its basketball and has nothing
   to do with one's growth,
But it's like everything when you look at one
   part the most.
What made you get out of bed and start your
   day?
What held your dreams and success along the
   way?
When it didn't work out, were you just a lost
   soul?
Or did it teach you to follow another goal?

When the talent was gone, did you just sit and
    cry?
Or because it was gone, did you give something
    else a try?
Or did it teach that same purpose in life,
Or was it just an old hoop on a board full of
    strife?
If that's what you see, it's worth nothing at all
Because in the end you'd see only a ball...
Not the dreams that you'd seek, with often no end,
For those are for dreamers and I dare not say when.
But I glance in the mirror, and what do I see...
Hard work and dreams that define what was me...
Not just a dreamer who hopes to achieve,
In order to do that, I had to BELIEVE.

This morning, I looked in the mirror and didn't see me,
I saw *Believe to Achieve* tacked to that tree.
My possible dream was there...I could see,
Believe to Achieve is how I became me.

The
Apprentice

BOOK ONE

The Outer Handbook

Any road will get you there
if you don't know where you're going.

My Moms used to tell us, "Any road will get you there if you don't know where you're going," and I pass this on for you to think about. It's important to know where you're going in life. If you don't, it might take you twenty years to get somewhere that would have only taken twenty minutes if you'd known what you wanted. So the trick is to figure out what it is that you really want.

When I was in college, I read an interview with Lamar Hunt in a magazine called *Success Unlimited*. His father, H. L. Hunt, had become a multibillionaire back before it was popular to be even a millionaire. The interviewer asked Mr. Hunt how his father was able to amass so much money. Hunt replied, "It was quite easy." The interviewer responded that it wasn't easy to put together large sums of money; it wasn't easy to put together *small* sums of money. So how could it be easy to put together billions of dollars? Mr. Hunt said his father's philosophy had always been that you first must have a vision. You must see what you really want and see it crystal clear. Second, you have to decide what you're willing to sacrifice to make it happen, what you'll be willing to give up to make your vision come true. Finally, you have to just go about the business of making it happen—or, as I tell young men and ladies in "Nike language": Just Do It.

When I speak to young people I always tell the H. L. Hunt story to inspire them. I still tell the story because I truly believe that these principles work. I have seen them in action again and again in my own life and in the lives of those around me. If you follow these three steps—vision, sacrifice, and doing the work—you can have anything you truly want out of life.

I adopted H. L. Hunt's philosophy, but I've added a fourth step to the process: Write down whatever it is that you want to accomplish so you'll have a reference point as you go forward.

ONE

Vision

People often ask me how I have been able to accomplish the things I have. The first thing I had to learn was how to think big.

5

I was in the eighth grade at the beginning of integration. There was a high school down the street that was open after school. Kecoughtan High had been a white school, but now with integration anyone could attend. One afternoon, some friends and I rode our bikes to the school. In the gym were four white men. They asked us if we wanted to play basketball with them.

Now, the way we played basketball in our neighborhood was quite different from the way these guys played. You'd have thought you were looking at two different games. They had very different rules. When we played, we just got the ball and shot; they had to take it back behind the free throw line. Consequently, for most of the game they had to stop and explain to us what we were supposed to do. Their version did make more sense. It simulated playing whole court basketball.

After the game, one of the men stopped and asked me my name. He told me he was Jim Hathaway, the coach at the high school. He then asked me if I had ever heard of Oscar Robertson. I said, "Yes, Sir!" while thinking to myself, Who hasn't? At that time, asking people if they knew the "Big O" was like asking people today if they know who Michael Jordan is. Coach Hathaway then said, "If you listen to everything I tell you, you can be just like the 'Big O.'"

Now, at this point I should tell you I'd been prone to going in the wrong direction—and even to shooting at the wrong basket. This white man was telling me that I could be just like the "Big O." How crazy could he be? Well, I thought he was stupid, so I decided to play stupid too. With nothing to lose, I listened

Start of the basketball journey, as a guard for the Kecoughtan Warriors.

to him. My motivation from that day on was to become like the "Big O." Coach Hathaway taught me how to "think" the game of basketball. He taught me how to dribble, shoot, pass, and play defense. He taught me how to really play the game. I eventually played for him at his school, and I became an All-American.

Basketball earned me the scholarship that paid my way through college. On the back of my college uniform I wore only the letter "H." Now most of the people who know me call me "H." That single letter has been my driving force since the days when I was in junior high school. I still hear those words: *If you listen to everything I tell you, you can be just like the "Big O."* Even when I stopped playing basketball, striving to be the "Big O" meant being the very best I could be, regardless of the specific goal. It helped me learn that I could reach for anything.

When you have a plan that you're willing to work toward, you never know where it might take you. Phil Knight started what has become a thirty-five-billion-dollar business out of the back of a station wagon. He was an accountant, but he wanted to sell shoes—so he did it out of the back of his car. His dad told him that he was crazy and not to quit his "safe" job, but he had a vision. He was an athlete and he wanted to make shoes that gave athletes an edge in sports. He and his track coach at the University of Oregon had a dream that they could make shoes with great traction. Coach Bowerman put a rubber compound in his wife's waffle iron one Sunday morning; the waffle sole came out, and the first waffle-sole trainer was born. Phil first imported Tiger shoes, then started a small company named Blue Ribbon Sports. He held a contest and one of his employees came up with the name Nike, which, appropriately, means the Goddess of Victory.

And-I Lesson

You need an image in your mind that you can hold up and work toward. Many of us are lucky enough to have people in our lives who tell us every day that we have something special about us. We can choose to listen to that truth or decide instead to listen to the negatives that come at us from all sides. I know you can fly now. All that's left for you to do is to flap your wings!

... the journey begins ...

TWO

Goal Setting

Moses Malone was the first basketball player to go from high school to the pros. In high school Moses averaged 36 points, 25 rebounds, and 12 blocked shots a game. He was a phenomenal player by any definition. When I was a college basketball coach, I recruited Moses to come to the University of Maryland. He signed with the university but never played a game there. Moses told me that when he was in junior high school, he had written down that he wanted to be the first player to go from high school to play in the NBA. He placed his note in his Bible, and that was the goal that he worked toward every day. I've always remembered that. Moses had a goal, he wrote it down, and he put it somewhere very special to him where he could refer to it.

One thing for sure in life is that everybody wants something. They may not know what it is as clearly as Moses did, but they do want something and the desire eats away at them. Everyone wants to be someone special. But only you can define what "special" means for you. This is a difficult task for many people. They just don't seem to know how to reach their goal.

As H. L. Hunt would say, the first thing you need is to have a vision and see it crystal clear. If you tell me that you have not defined your goals, what you're really saying is that you don't know what you want to do or what you want to become. To set realistic goals, keep the following steps in mind:

- **DON'T START WITH PLANS THAT ARE TOO BIG.** *The ultimate goal can be big, but the plans need to build up to it. When I wanted to be the "Big O," I didn't plan on trying out for the Cincinnati Royals that week, but I pushed myself to get better for my own team.*

- **THINK ABOUT WHAT IT IS THAT YOU REALLY WANT.** *What is important to you? Is it helping people? Doing something that no one else has done before? Following in the footsteps of someone you admire? Don't settle for a casual or superficial answer.*

- **THINK ABOUT WHAT IT IS THAT YOU DO WELL.** *Maybe there is something that you do a little better than your friends. Or maybe there is something that you just love to do that gives you great joy.*

I'm sure you know the second step already and are yelling it out now. It's the thing that will make you like Moses Malone: *Write it down!* Put it in a place where you can find it and refer to it when needed. This might sound crazy but it works. Just give it a try and see. Nothing beats a failure but a try.

The third thing you must do is to decide what you are willing to sacrifice, or what you must give up, to make your dream happen. This is an important part of the equation; it may even be the hardest part. Remember: everyone wants something, but many don't realize that nothing comes for free, so they aren't willing to give up anything to get what they want.

The fourth step is to go about the business of making it happen.

Finally, don't get discouraged by the obstacles that get in your way. Every experience offers a lesson to be learned and gives you an opportunity to grow and get closer to your goal. Life actually is a bed of roses, but there will always be thorns in the brier patch.

A friend at Nike told me that every birthday since he was ten years old, all he had wanted was a Porsche. Whenever anyone asked him what he wanted for his birthday, he'd say, "A Porsche." Although he'd received a lot of toy and model Porsches throughout his life, he still knew that it was what he wanted. On his fortieth birth-day he went out and bought a Porsche. He had worked and saved and finally had what he needed to get his dream. All of those years of wanting and visualizing had finally paid off.

The mind is the most powerful thing in the universe. It is where all things begin and end. It is through this power of the mind that you can make your true dreams come to life. Really think about the vast power of the brain and the tiny amount of it that we use. I've wondered why some people produce more than others do. I think it is simply because they use more of their mental power. If it weren't for thought, there would be no cars, radios, cities, and so forth. Someone had to think of them. Someone had to dream them.

There are those of us who simply think, letting thoughts come and go, and then there are those who think and act upon their thoughts. I hope this book will stimulate both thought and action. I want you to be a person who acts upon those things that come into your mind. The problem that many of us encounter is that we can't focus on what it is that we truly want. We watch others do things and then we say, "I could have done that." If you could have done it, you should have been doing it. Dare to be great. Even better: Dare to be happy. I'm not saying that you have to go out and build a bridge to Europe or a link to Mars. But I am saying that you shouldn't just sit around and do nothing. Life is an action plan, and you have the tools to put it in action now. The key word here is *now*!

One of my greatest dreams to come true was the creation of Nike's Jordan brand. The greatest things in life generally start as ideas that have to be sold to someone else, and at first, no one wants to buy. People can be slow to take to new ideas. The Wright brothers believed that man could fly. People laughed at them, and they had plenty of failures to overcome before they created a plane that flew. Where would we be today if they had given up? I felt that Air Jordan could stand alone as a separate brand; not many other people believed in that idea. I fought and fought for Michael to have his own brand. It took about five years but it finally happened. On the heels of hard work, focus, concentration, and belief, anything in the world is possible.

It seems that the ills of life are received with less persuasion. People tend to search out the bad things. They somehow go out and find drugs, alcohol, and unsafe sex. Those don't have to be sold—but there's also no long-term benefit. For the things you

M. J. and H at a Nike photo shoot in 1984, with the shoe
that started it all.

believe in, the road is tougher. Never let your dreams
die. You may have to sell them, but there is always
someone willing to buy if you are tenacious. Spread your
wings, believe in yourself, and fly.

And-I Lesson

Let's review your goal-setting plans.
Have a clear vision. We'll call it:

1. Visualize
Think about what you want in school, in work, and
in your personal life. Then put it somewhere
so you can refer to it to keep you on your path.

2. Write It Down
Next, decide what you must give up to make it happen.

3. Sacrifice
Then go about the business of making it happen.

4. Do the Work
Finally, don't worry about the obstacles
that life throws in your way.

5. Always Know
there will be thorns in the brier patch.

THREE

Make It Happen

Try not. Do. Or do not. There is no try.

—Yoda, from *The Empire Strikes Back*

SACRIFICE

Everyone wants something, but not everyone is willing
to recognize that they have to give to get. There are
no free lunches in life. I'm sure you've heard this many
times, but if this is your first time, let me tell you once more:
There are no free lunches in life! Everything has a price tag.

It may sound simple, but sacrifice is one of the most difficult
things in the world. People have visions and dreams every day,
but the fact that you have to give up something you enjoy to make
something else happen means that many of those dreams won't
come to pass. The average person has a problem with deferred
gratification. People generally want what they want right now—
whether it is the right thing to have at the time or not. What they
don't realize is that they're sacrificing anyway. They sacrifice
long-term satisfaction or happiness for short-term pleasure. If you
can overcome this habit, you will be well on your way to success.

15

I'm writing this book to show you that hard work does pay off. If you keep your eye on your goal and never lose faith in yourself, there's nothing you can't accomplish! Sometimes this will mean waking up an hour earlier than usual and going over your homework or a presentation for your job to ensure that you're prepared for the day ahead. Other times it will mean giving up something fun so you can save the money to buy equipment or something you need for your business. Still other times it will mean practicing (shooting baskets, going over a math problem, trying new marketing strategies, and so forth) twice as hard as the next person. But if you keep your eyes on the prize, and practice, practice, practice, you will develop the habits necessary to succeed at anything you want. No matter what happens to you, you are the one in control of how you prepare yourself.

DO THE WORK

When you see Michael Jordan hit a last-second shot, that's not the first time he has hit it. He's shot it millions of times. He shot it in the backyard as he was growing up. He shot before and after practice millions of times, and he shot it in his mind millions upon millions of times. To become the best takes a lot of practice and hard work. But if you put a lot of practice and hard work into anything you do, you will become the best you can be. That is all anyone can ever ask of you—that you become the best that you can possibly be. You won't know how good you can be unless you put your all into the things that you pursue. If you want to become one of the best lawyers the world has ever seen, you have to put in more time than anyone else. You might want to be a great doctor. Then start at the bottom and be willing to work hard. Be about the business of a successful you.

During one of Nike's Believe to Achieve seminars, in which I go out and speak to young people, I was listening to one of the other speakers, Peter Bynoe. Peter is not the biggest guy in the world physically, but he is big in stature in the field of business. Peter was the first black to own an NBA basketball team. He put a group together and bought the Denver Nuggets. All of the players love and appreciate him and his accomplishments. When he spoke to the seminar group he said that buying the team wasn't the most important thing to him but giving a deserving fellow black person a chance to be the general manager was. Peter is also the person who built Cominsky Park in Chicago, where the Chicago White Sox play their home games. This is a huge accomplishment by anyone's standards. When he spoke about this, he said that Cominsky Park was nice, but the most important thing about the project was that he displaced eighty-one families, and getting to build them new homes was the most rewarding part of the deal.

Now, what really got my attention was when Peter told the audience that as a young man he decided he wasn't the smartest guy in school but that nothing could keep him from being the hardest working person in school. Now, we are talking about someone who went to Harvard and Harvard Law School and is on several boards of directors, including one at Harvard. He said, "I don't have to be the smartest person, but I will be the hardest working person here." This is advice that we all can follow. After this seminar I felt that I too could do more.

When you find what it is that you are supposed to be doing, you put all of your passion and zest for life into it. This is how you become an extraordinary person, which is only an ordinary person on fire with desire. The important part of this is the *extra*. So, you can be ordinary but put some *extra* into it.

HABITS

Habits are those things that you do every day without even thinking about them. If you get in the bed from the left side when you're young, chances are that you'll get in from the left when you are older as well. Habits are hard to break. There are good and bad habits; the good ones are usually harder to form, whereas the bad ones, like smoking or drinking, often may make you feel good. If you don't start bad habits, you won't have to break them. It's always better to start forming good habits when you're young, but you can form them at any time.

Any improvement that you decide to make needs your commitment to become a habit. You can't start something new, perform it twice a month, and expect it to become part of you. You must drill yourself constantly and diligently to make it a habit, and only then will it have an effect on your life. And you must constantly replace discouraging, negative messages with positive messages.

I must caution you: if you increase the time you spend on something but retain bad habits that aren't helping you, you will probably not see any improvements. If you find that you just can't break out of your old ways of doing things, then it's time to look for help—from a friend, counselor, coworker, or family member. Everyone who achieves greatness gets help along the way. Though you can't do everything by yourself, you can still take charge of finding someone to help you.

Maybe the most important habit is staying caught up. You can undermine your own schedule by not preparing for things in advance. Don't wait for the last minute—do it now! Saying you'll "get to it later" is procrastination. "Later" comes, and it's still not done. You have a calendar; so use it to stay ahead of the game. Staying caught up puts you in control of one of the most important things you possess—your time.

AND-I LESSON

How much is it worth to you, to accomplish your dream? Is it worth saving money for? Or spending time on? Think about the steps you can take every day to move closer to your goal. Think about your habits. Are they the things that will help you on your way?

Sacrifice can be hard, but making your life special is really quite easy. All you need is a clear goal and to do the work it takes. The road may be full of potholes, and you may have to change a flat tire, but you can get there.

FOUR

Best Foot Forward

I can't give you fortune and fame,
but you do have a name. Take care of it.
— Lillian M. White

At a summer basketball game right before I finished
college, Dr. J—the great basketball player Julius Irving—
asked me if I had gotten my degree or if I was on time
to get it. I said that I should be getting it pretty soon.
Dr. J said, "Howard, you really want to get that degree
as soon as possible, because they forget who you are pretty
quickly after you finish playing ball." That stayed in my mind,
and I got my degree that summer. Around that time, Coach
Driesell asked me if I wanted to stay on at Maryland as an
assistant coach. He didn't want a résumé; he just asked me to
write a paper on why I wanted to become a coach at Maryland
and the reasons why he should hire me. I had never really
thought about being a coach, but I gave it some serious thought.
And I decided that this seemed like it would be a really good
thing to do. I felt that I could bring something to the Maryland
program.

Coach Driesell and H with statue of Testudo the Terrapin, University of Maryland's mascot.

So, I became an assistant basketball coach and also the assistant intramural director at the University of Maryland. That was pretty sweet. I recruited some of the greatest ball players in the country. I recruited the likes of Moses Malone, who was the best high school player I'd ever seen.

I loved to meet prospective players, recruit them, and learn about who they were and what made them the best. I was also interested in what type of family they came from and just what made them so special. It was usually something quite intangible. It was that part of them that beat underneath their skin and really couldn't be measured; it's called Heart. Heart isn't exclusive to sports. It's found everywhere. It's what separates the person who is good at what they do from just another person at the table of life.

The Apprentice

A couple of years ago, Coach Driesell asked me to speak at his basketball banquet at Georgia State University. When he introduced me, I heard for the first time why he had hired me to be a coach at the University of Maryland. He said that he had watched me throughout my basketball career at Maryland, and he had been impressed by my strong work ethic and honesty and how the other players followed me. He also said that he hadn't had a job available but he had really wanted me to be a part of his staff, so he created a position for me. Coach and I didn't always see eye-to-eye on everything, but he realized that I believed in the things for which I fought. He had seen that I could do a job I had never thought about, when I didn't even know he was paying attention.

The lesson here: You never know when people are watching you. Therefore, always put your best foot forward.

ATTITUDE

Putting your best foot forward also means seeing the best side of things. Take life by the hand and lead it where you want to go. You may not control what happens to you, but you are in control of how you live your life, and your attitude will determine the outcome. This is your buffer against the world. Have a cheery outlook and a positive attitude. Why be negative about anything when you can just as easily be positive? Be positive in the way you carry yourself. People will sense your positive attitude and will most likely act in kind. If they don't, don't let them stop you or steal your sunshine. Keep your head high and move on.

Attitude is one of your most important assets in life. This is simply the way you see things and your approach toward them. See the good in things and in yourself. Do you take a negative approach or a positive approach to everything you do? You do have a choice in this matter. A smile on your face will always work better than a frown. Remember this very important tip: You get one chance, and one chance only, to make a first impression on someone. You'd better make it a great one. This may be the person who one day gives you the greatest job in the world. This may be your future wife or husband. Have a great outlook on life—it doesn't cost anything.

The great thing about an attitude is that you can carry it with you. No matter what is going on or where you're going, you can take your attitude. A positive attitude helps the world and the people in it. A negative attitude hurts the world and hurts you even more. If you're busy lifting up the world, it will never be able to let you down. You can control your attitude toward anything and everything that comes into your world.

See your life as a glass full of water, with a pile of pennies next to it. The pennies are positive thoughts, and what you want to do is replace the water in the jar with pennies. The first one you drop in is nothing more than a penny in a glass of water. It simply goes in and settles to the bottom of the glass, barely visible. But each day you drop in additional pennies. If you drop them in morning, noon, and night, it will take a while, but soon the pennies will begin to displace the water. As you put in more and more pennies, the water will start to spill out of the glass. At the end you will have a glass full of pennies and the water will be gone. There will be no room left in your life for anything but positive thoughts.

TWICE SAID

One thing that Moms did teach us children was that each and every person that we come in contact with deserves to be treated with respect. The only way that you will ever get respect in life is if you give it. Now, you shouldn't worry about if and when it will come back to you—your job is to give it.

Sometimes people say things that stick with us and carry us through life. If we are fortunate we may hear them more than once—if we listen close enough. There was something that I only heard Moms say twice. The first time we were walking down the street on a Saturday morning. We passed by one of the older men in the neighborhood, Mr. Lee, who walked with a noticeable limp. Mr. Lee and Moms spoke to each other.

25

"How are you today, Lee?"

"I'm fine, Lillian. How are you?"

I just kept walking and picking up and throwing rocks—what most boys nine or ten years old would be doing, I guess. But after we passed by Mr. Lee, she said, "Let that be the last time you walk by someone and don't open your mouth. Even a dog can wag its tail when it passes you on the street." For some reason that stuck with me.

About six months before Moms passed away, I asked her: What would she like her grandchildren and their children to remember about her? She paused for a bit and said, "I really know how to treat people. Even a dog can wag its tail when it passes you on the street."

It was only twice said, but never forgotten.

AND-I LESSON

Even a dog can wag its tail when it passes you on the street. So, never walk past anyone without saying hello. It doesn't cost anything to say good morning or good evening. Period! No ifs, ands, or buts about it.

Don't displace your dreams with negative thoughts. When Michael Jordan returned to basketball from retirement, he faced enormous challenges—and went on to win three more championships. His character is such that he thrives on adversity. He is capable of turning any negative situation around to make it positive and give himself the edge. Look for situations that can give you an edge. If the playing field isn't balanced, do what you can to swing it to your favor. No one said it would be easy, but you can make it happen.

FIVE

Responsibility

At some point, we may think that we can do things and
not be held accountable for them. What we eventually
learn is that we never actually do anything to anyone
else—we only do it to ourselves. I know that sounds
crazy, and you probably think that I've taken leave of
my senses. Hear my story, though, before you decide that
I've lost it completely and put this book down forever.

27

As a sixth grader, I was a safety patrol officer. I got to wear
a bright orange patrol belt. Mrs. Hall was my teacher at that
time, and she was extremely tough. The truth was that I was very
proud to become a patrol boy under her watchful eye. We were
the keepers of the flock. We assisted the crossing guards at the
end of the school day; we monitored the halls. The belt meant
that we had responsibility. And the belt taught me a very important lesson in life.

One day, Mrs. Hall had to leave the room. The students
were working quietly and everything was going well. Then one

of the guys in the class started yelling at one of the girls. He shouted something that was very inappropriate, but it was also very funny. We all started laughing and having a great time. Although the girl was embarrassed and near tears, most of us found the boy's comments hilarious and continued to laugh. But it wasn't funny to all of us.

Just when we were nearly in tears with laughter, Mrs. Hall walked back into the classroom. Everyone immediately stopped and got back to work. Mrs. Hall sensed something, and asked what was going on. Leona raised her hand and said exactly what William had said to her. Mrs. Hall asked him to come to the front of the room and tell her just what he'd said. He tried to make it sound like something quite different. Now, he was on punishment. He had to hold out his hand and feel the sting of the ruler. He had to stay after school as well. Mrs. Hall then instructed me to come to the front of the room. She jerked the patrol belt off of me so fast I didn't have time to react. I stood there like a fool until she told me I could take my seat. Everyone looked but they didn't say anything. I guess the last laugh was on me. Humiliated! In the sixth grade, this was a fate worse than death.

Some lessons last a lifetime. You can be a part of the problem or you can be a part of the solution. I had been a part of the problem.

There is no action without a reaction. Everything you do or think has an impact somewhere else in the universe. Sometimes you see the consequences right away, sometimes not. But either way, there's no such thing as "getting away with it." At some point it will come back to you.

As long as we hold someone else accountable for what we do, we don't grow. We stagnate. Parents, guardians, partners, friends, coworkers—none of them are responsible for us. Until you accept responsibility for yourself, you can't prepare yourself for anything in life. People who enter into adolescence this way grow into adulthood unprepared for responsible living. How can you become a responsible person in the world if you've never taken responsibility for yourself? It is never too early to take responsibility for your actions—or too late. We are the masters of our universe, which simply means that we are the masters of ourselves.

It was the fifth game of the 1996 World Championship series between the Chicago Bulls and the Seattle Supersonics. The Bulls had won the first two games in Chicago pretty easily. They then went to Seattle for three games on the Supersonics' home court. The Bulls won the first game in Seattle by quite a few points. They were feeling very confident. Then Seattle won the fourth game and went on to have an easy fifth game win. This Championship drive had come on the heels of a season of seventy-two wins and only ten losses for the Chicago Bulls—the most wins in a season by any team in the history of the NBA! After the Bulls lost that second game, all of Michael Jordan's friends who had come to Seattle for the game were in his hotel room. The conversation was neither healthy nor positive. Everyone began to cast doubt by discussing the seemingly unthinkable fate of losing the Championship.

"None of the other guys want to win bad enough."

"No one is playing good defense."

"No one is doing anything right."

I couldn't believe what my ears were hearing. I remembered the patrol belt. I could be part of the problem or I could be part of the solution. I yelled out, "You're all insane! These are the same guys you've just won seventy-two games with! They haven't changed one bit! If you could win seventy-two games I'm sure you can find a way to win just one more!" The Bulls went back to Chicago and won their fourth NBA Championship that year. I couldn't let the negative talk continue. If it persisted, there was a chance that people would buy into it. I remembered the lesson from Mrs. Hall.

AND-I LESSON

It's just this simple: Whatever actions you take in life, be responsible for them. Don't hold other people responsible for the things that you do. You do have a chance to make a difference! It's your choice. You can be part of the problem or you can be part of the solution!

SIX

Change

If there is one certainty in life, it is that everything must change. At some point, sooner or later, change will occur. And change is good. When accepted, change is typically followed by personal or professional growth. Your best bet is to view change as something positive and approach it in the same manner. Most people take a negative approach to change; what ends up happening is that the change controls them. They become pawns on a chessboard. To be the master of the game, you must have a positive outlook on change.

If you can control your emotions and embrace new situations, you will remain in control of yourself. If you can do this, you will be way ahead of the game. Always remember: change *will* come. It's how you receive it that will determine how far you can take it (or how far it can take you).

When I was in junior high school, my girlfriend asked me to change schools, because her mother wanted her to transfer from the school we were then attending. I thought this was a great idea because at this new school I'd have her all to myself. My mother allowed me to transfer to attend the new school. On the first day of classes, I didn't see her anywhere—and something else was different. The school to which I had transferred was 98 percent white. There were almost no black students (to be exact, there were three of us).

When I got home and called her to see where she'd been, I found out that she had transferred to a different school! I never did understand exactly what had happened, but I was now in this all-white school, and the very reason that I had changed schools was now a joke. I knew that my mother would not allow me to change schools a second time. I was stuck in this predominantly white school without my girlfriend. I had to sink or swim.

This was change at its worst. I felt the weight of the entire world on my shoulders. I embraced the situation and turned it completely around. I got to play basketball on the team. The teachers treated me well and gave me a great deal of encouragement. I made some wonderful new friends who I still keep in touch with today.

Upon leaving the school after my ninth-grade year, I was voted "Most Popular Student." This all came from the change in my life. I could have complained and made it the worst thing in my life, but I accepted it and made it something special. I've always wanted to thank that young lady for asking me to change schools. That one incident changed the course of my life. It set me on a path that has been nothing short of a miracle.

Some things you can control, some you can't. That's another important thing to remember about change. You may have your vision and set your goals and be working toward them, and then your circumstances change and you have to start over. Maybe a school program is cut, or you have an injury that won't let you perform the way you planned. That can be discouraging, but it's important to remember that you can always control how you react to change. And when circumstances change, you can alter your goals to fit them. When one door closes, another opens. If you stay open to change and let go of those things you can't control, you will eventually end up with something even better than what you could have imagined.

The important thing is not to settle but to push forward and not blame circumstances for whether you succeed or not. People often think that life must be easy for those stars who have lots of money. Or they say, "If I'd had what he had, I could have done anything I wanted to do," or "I didn't get the chance that she got," or "If someone had given me an opportunity I would be great today." Everyone has the opportunity to be great! You can create the opportunities for yourself—even if you've been dealt the worst hand in the deck.

I use the stories of athletes to inspire and move you because you know and respect them already. Sure, the likes of Tiger Woods, Cynthia Cooper, Lisa Leslie, Marion Jones, and Michael Vick are all very inspiring. But I have met inspiring people in every walk of life. I recently met a young man by the name of

33

Rudy Garcia-Tolson, who let me know not in words but by his presence that this book is right on target. Rudy is about fourteen years of age and a wonderful person. He's just someone that you feel good being around. Michael Jordan is one of his heroes, and when he was visiting with me I called Michael and Rudy got to speak to him.

As Rudy was leaving he gave me a card with his picture, and he asked me to give it to Michael. On the card he had written, "To MJ, Never Give Up!!!! All My Best! Rudy." Now, here is a fourteen-year-old telling Michael Jordan to never give up! That might seem ludicrous, until you learn that Rudy was born with a rare disease and is a double amputee. There was Rudy in shorts, standing on his artificial legs and wearing a pair of Air Jordans, with the greatest attitude in the world. A wonderful sense of humor, a winning smile—and he's just plain fun to be around.

What is even more amazing is that Rudy runs a mile in a little over six minutes. He can run a 5K in 20.08 minutes. When he works out he swims 5,000 meters, and he holds the American 200-meter breaststroke record for his class. He also rides a bike that was built especially for him. So you see, he could tell Michael Jordan never to give up. He *really* knows something about challenge. Rudy let me see that regardless of who or where we are in life, it's simply up to each of us— and it's all right there inside of us, waiting for us to let it out. Rudy's motto is "A brave heart is a powerful weapon." So tell me: What can't you do? In each person lies a seed that is so powerful it can break through anything that tries to hold it in. May your flower bloom.

And-I Lesson

Even if something doesn't go the way you want it to, look for the hidden gift. When the unexpected happens, it brings new opportunities with it. If you can see far enough, you can see that the sun is still shining, even if it's a cloudy day. It's up above the clouds somewhere, all you need to do is find it. Embrace change and you will see your life and dreams take off and soar like an eagle!

35

SEVEN

Mentors

In my professional life, I mentor superstars and world-famous CEOs. I mentor both famous people and people just like you and me. People seek my advice and I guide them along their road. I do this because I've had many people help me though the years, and I know how important it is to pass along what you've learned.

After I failed the second grade, my next teacher, Mrs. Vaughn, let me know from day one what she expected. She also told me that she knew I could do it. When I transferred schools, my eighth-grade English teacher told me that I was special because I was a wonderful poet. Coach Hathaway told me that I could be just like the "Big O." My high school English teachers made me work to earn each grade that I received. So many people saw more in me than I was capable of seeing in myself. They also believed in me. Because

37

of their continued support and encouragement, I couldn't let them down.

In college, Dr. Charlotte Leedy asked me to stay after class one day. She told me that she had only met two students in her life who were gifted enough to command the attention of an entire class. She said the first young man was from Philadelphia, whom she'd had in class when she taught at Temple University. The other was Howard White. She said that the only difference between us was that he was from Philadelphia. When he spoke, people understood him. Being from Virginia, I spoke with a strong southern accent. People didn't always understand what I was saying. She told me she had a friend who was a speech teacher on campus. She wanted me to spend some time with her. I did this and it made a difference in my speaking ability. Thank you, Dr. Leedy, for seeing something I couldn't see for myself.

Mentoring can happen at any age, in any field, and at any level. Just as Coach Hathaway taught me the ins and outs of basketball, Phil Knight has taught me the ins and outs of corporate culture. He has exposed me to high-level meetings involving millions of dollars. The lessons he has taught me are invaluable. In the real world of business, corporate waters are shark infested, so you need people who are capable of helping you swim to shore. As a black man in corporate America you have to give it all you have because the odds are sometimes stacked against you. It doesn't hurt to have someone of Mr. Knight's stature to call on for advice.

When the people in charge are your friends, it can sometimes make your job harder, because people expect that you'll use the friendship card for everything. They expect you to run to that person, avoiding protocol to make things happen. But the deal is, you don't use a relationship to get ahead. You owe it to that person to give your very best all the time, to make them proud of you. I always wanted Coach Hathaway to be proud of me because of the time he put into my development; I always wanted Moms to be proud of me because she put so much time and effort into raising me. Phil fit right into this equation. I think he came into my life so that I could relay this story to you, so that you could discover that you can "see it, believe it, achieve it." I know this can work for you if you truly believe in yourself and seek out others who believe in you too. You have the power within yourself if you can visualize what you

Phil Knight and H at a celebration honoring Nelson Mandela with a Civil Rights Freedom Award.

want out of life. Mr. Knight believed in me; he gave me inspiration and let me know I had special talent. I don't know why I was someone whom he believed in, but he did. I think everyone has someone who believes in him or her. Everyone has a Coach Hathaway or a Phil Knight. We have people all around us; we just have to see who they are.

Walking on a path by the ocean in Hawaii one day, I saw a beautiful figure carved into a tree. The work was so beautiful that it caught my eye immediately. A man with a beard sat beside the figure, and I asked the man if he'd done the carving. He looked at me and then said that he had just let the figure out of the wood. It had been there all along—he had just released it. He had seen something in the wood that not many people were capable of seeing. He had simply let the man out! He had freed the figure from within the tree. So many of us are still hidden inside our tree. Others seek to set us free; allow them to chisel away!

AND-I LESSON

Find people who will mentor you. Perhaps your mentors are teachers, coaches, ministers, coworkers, aunts, or uncles. These are people you respect, people you can look up to and go to for advice. They have the ability to give you a different perspective. Try to look for positive people so their influence is both positive and uplifting. Mentors are everywhere. Listen to yours!

EIGHT

Rules of the Game

★

Life is a game. The better you hope to be at it, the more thoroughly you need to know the rules. Until you know the rules of the game, you will never play to your full potential. No matter who your hero is—Tiger Woods, LeBron James, Lisa Leslie, Serena Williams—I assure you that they know the rules of the game extremely well. Michael Jordan, who many say is the best player to ever play basketball, knows the rules of his game very well. He studied them just like referees study them. He had to know them so he could know just how far he could walk on the edge. In business, you must know just how far you can go before you are out of bounds. It's OK to be different, but you must know where the edges are. Deion Sanders is one of the best cornerbacks ever to play football. He isn't just talented; he knows exactly what he can and can't do. This allows him to get the most out of his talent. If he makes an error, he studies that too and figures out how to avoid it the next time.

What would a world without rules be like? Would it be fun to live in? I think it would be a world exclusively for the rich and powerful. There would be no middle ground. You'd have a lot or nothing. You could only work for the rich and powerful, and they'd do with you as they pleased. A fun world? I don't think so. Rules give everyone a chance to be someone. People can learn the rules and then work on improving their game. What would a game be like without rules? The word that comes to mind is "chaos."

Life is sort of like a marching band. You can be an individual, but you still must stay in step with your band. You can be the drum major and do all of the wild and crazy things they do, but you still must know the rules. If you want to lead, you have to work hard to know what everyone else is doing so you can make the entire unit work well together. You can high-step and kick, but you still have to be in step. You must follow rules to be in step with the world, but if you know the rules you can walk the edges with precision and style and be better than you even know.

DISCIPLINE

At the heart of this book there is an exercise that I truly believe in. It's the simple task of making up your bed every morning. If you're like my daughter, Mandy, you will ask, "Why?" Because it leaves your house and world a better place. But more importantly, it's a good habit. It creates discipline, and discipline is an important part of life.

Let's look at a story of two dogs. Dog number one was very free as a puppy; his owner just let him do whatever he wanted. His owner let him jump up on the furniture; when visitors came over he jumped up on them. Sometimes he was told "no," sometimes not.

Dog number two was disciplined all the time as a puppy. He wasn't allowed up on the furniture. He wasn't allowed to jump on visitors when they came into the house. It was hard to do, but the second owner made it a habit to be responsible and ensure that the puppy learned all of these things. "No" meant "no," and the owner would make sure that it was said in a timely fashion. It was a lot harder to be owner number two; all of his time seemed to be spent making sure the puppy did what he was supposed to.

Time went on and both dogs grew up. Dog number one wasn't as free as he had been when he was a puppy. He got spanked often but still didn't pay attention. He was too big to get up on the furniture. He wouldn't listen when he went outside and would run away. So, dog number one spent most of his time in a cage or tied to a chain.

Dog number two was a well-behaved dog. He got to run in the park with his master. He got to stay in the house because he listened. He went for long walks because he knew how to walk on a leash. In effect, dog number one, who'd had lots of freedom as a puppy, had no freedom as a grown-up. Dog number two, who was disciplined as a puppy, had lots of freedom later on. That's how life works. Having discipline creates other opportunities for you. Making up your bed every day is the first step to creating discipline in your life.

AND-I LESSON

Be an active student of life. Learn all you can. You can't be on the edge if you don't know the rules of the game. The starting point is making up your bed in the morning. A foundation of discipline will give you the freedom to explore new horizons.

NINE

Strength

★

There was a long blast from a car horn. We went outside to see what was the matter. My dad's car was in
the driveway, and Dad was slumped over the steering
wheel. We saw blood. Moms saw that Daddy was
still breathing and told us to get him into the house.
We got him in and Moms started to patch him up. He
wanted to go back to wherever he'd been, to get back at whoever
had shot him. My mother was quite calm and didn't pay much
attention to what Daddy wanted. The wound wasn't that bad—
the bullet had gone through his side. Moms mended Dad's
wounds; he finally calmed down and didn't go anywhere but to
bed.

The strength that Moms showed was exceptional. In all my
life, I never once heard that lady complain. Not even after my
dad left us and we had to move out of that house that I remember best from childhood. Not that it was such a great house, but
it was where all of my friends and memories were: skating up

45

and down the street, early morning fishing trips, church outings, and bingo on Sunday evenings with the family. Dad left to go across town to live with another family when I was about twelve years old. We moved in with my aunts and after a while moved into public housing. I never once heard Moms say anything negative about anything. Her life was work and family. I know she sacrificed a great deal to make things work for us. When we moved to the country she walked miles to the bus stop. She'd walk there early in the morning and walk back late at night. Yet she always wore a smile.

My mother cleaned houses for a living. She was a very simple woman, yet she was the master of truth and honesty. She didn't have to say or do anything special. I just watched the way she lived her life. She led by example and showed me how to stand strong no matter what life dealt out.

IN THE MIDDLE OF THE BRIER PATCH

There are moments that test us all. There will be times that test everything you believe in. Life is just what it is. It isn't always a nice bed of roses, nor should it be. There are always some thorns too.

Ouch! One day at Nike I felt the thorns in the brier patch, and the prick was pretty bad. I was called into Phil Knight's office. I had been working for Phil, the Chief Executive Officer and cofounder of Nike, Inc., for twelve years.

Phil questioned me regarding a close friend of mine. As it turned out, he was really finding out about me. He talked about certain phone calls and former employees who now worked for Adidas. After he talked to me, I had to talk to the FBI. I couldn't believe my ears: I was being accused of being a traitor and giving information to the competition.

I've always been a very loyal employee. Phil Knight had been my advisor, my mentor. I had to ask, Why would someone think I'd do something against this man and his company? Nike wasn't just some huge corporation to me. When I thought of Nike, I thought of Phil and Penny Knight. My relationship with Nike was made personal through them; to me, Phil and Penny Knight *were* Nike. So if I did anything against Nike, I would be doing it against them.

I had to take a leave of absence to let the FBI conduct its investigation. This turn of events disturbed me, but I knew I hadn't done anything wrong. What made it hard for Donna, my wife, was that she knew I had a great deal of loyalty to Phil. But he had a company to run and sometimes that can be a very difficult task. Until you walk in someone else's shoes, you can't fully appreciate that person's world.

Not everything in life is simple. You have to take some lumps and bumps along the way if you want to get to the smooth part of the road. It would have been easy to react badly to the situation. Instead, I simply used the lessons that I'd learned all my life. This was the sort of moment for which I'd been born. This situation gave me a chance to let people see a little of my strength. I live my life so that I can stand up to the tests that are put before me. If I did otherwise, how would I know how good I was? Just how much do I believe the advice that so many people seek from me? If you spend your life preparing for a test, don't you want to take it? Sometimes getting to the middle of the brier patch can be difficult. You will get scraped and scratched. You may even bleed a little. But you will survive.

After the investigation was over, Phil told me that the reason for the drill was that Michael Jordan was getting more and more powerful, and I was Michael's power inside of Nike. I also had a very strong relationship with Phil himself and that made some people nervous. When it was all over, Phil said, "If you don't want to be with Nike anymore, you could take the largest settlement in the history of mankind." I told him that he'd asked me to come there to do a job, and it wasn't finished yet.

I was flying across the country some years ago, and one of the flight attendants found out that I worked for Nike. She told me that she had been in an accident several years earlier, and the doctor's prognosis had been that she might not ever walk again. She was lying in bed watching television when she saw a commercial with Bo Jackson, made right after his hip replacement surgery. In the ad he comes through a television and tells a boy watching the commercial that he has rehabilitation work to do. She said that it had been a slow process, but after seeing that ad she made up her mind that she would walk again. She did walk, and even run. She was training to run her first 10K. Now running daily, she credits her recovery to that commercial. She said she also had the words "Just Do It" tattooed on her butt.

Do I still work for the company? I'm the vice president of the Jordan Brand. Nike is my passion, which I try to share with people every chance I get. I know that what we at Nike have done has helped people work out more, become more physically fit, live longer, and reduce the stress in their lives. This is the Nike of which I am so proud. I've been with the company for twenty years but I've never sold shoes or apparel. What I've sold are hopes and dreams.

All precious things are guarded by something. They aren't just there for the taking. If you want diamonds, you have to mine them. Everyone can get to the berries on the outside of the patch. Birds eat them and anyone walking by can pick them. The ones that are protected are so much better. The big, juicy berries can be a lot of trouble, and you have to get some scratches to get them, but I will tell you they are worth the work. Taste the difference. Trust me on this—I'm living proof. After you taste the berries, you won't mind the thorns that scratch and scrape. In the middle of the brambles you'll find the sweetest berries. Good hunting.

49

THREE MAGIC WORDS

The important thing to remember at all times is that the stream is filled with bad twists and turns, and you must have the stamina to maneuver through the rough spots. When you make up your mind to do something, don't give up! Keep doing what needs to be done to achieve your goal.

Sometimes we seem to get the worst end of the stick, and many people end up feeling that life is ugly or that it's painful and unfair. The thorns are like sharp knives that tear them apart. Ironically, when we've been abused, we sometimes reach out to abuse others. Our reflex is to hurt because we've been hurt. The blunt truth is, life isn't always fair. To get us through the rough patches, we need magic in our lives.

What has gotten me through rough times are three "magic" words. These three magic words are "in spite of." "I will reach my goals and my dreams *in spite of* everything that happens to me. Nothing will stop me from achieving what I so richly deserve. *In spite of* anyone or anything that stands in my path, I will reach my destination."

These are words that an old man told me a long time ago. It was so long ago, I'm not even sure how I knew him. And I'm not sure why he picked me to share his wisdom with, but he did. Maybe he knew that I'd write this book so that you could feel the magic as well. Those words have given me strength more times than I can count. They can work magic in your life too.

AND-I LESSON

To make the magic work you may need to repeat the three magic words—"in spite of"—over and over.

Life can deal crushing blows, but you can still achieve your goals. The road is filled with people who have survived astonishing setbacks, and you can too. You can live through anything with dignity and courage. I know you can overcome any obstacle that may be placed before you.

TEN

Believe

★

BELIEVE IN YOUR DREAMS

If I told you that there was just one thing you could do that would give you everything you want, would you do it? Well, all you have to do is believe! All that matters is that you can see what you want and believe in it with all your heart and soul.

Michael Jordan owns many cars and most of them have special license plates. It was the night of the first game of the NBA Eastern Conference Finals; Chicago was playing the Indiana Pacers to see which team would go to the Champi-onship. Michael and I were getting into his Ferrari, leaving the house for the game. I looked at the license plate and couldn't figure out what it meant. It read "MJ5." I asked him what the MJ5 stood for. He looked at me and said, "Michael Jordan—5 championships, fool." As we drove, listening to the music he had selected to help relax him before the game, he suddenly looked over at me and said, "I have MJ6 on order already." He didn't say it in a cocky way. He just really believed that it would happen. Few people believe that strongly and still fewer work hard enough for their beliefs to reach fruition. He did win that sixth championship. How much do *you* believe?

Once in a high school game I was at half court and I saw one of my teammates, Edlo Peoples, cut under the basket and hold up his hand. The game was very tight and people were on the edge of their seats. It was late in the game and we needed a basket. I passed the ball to Edlo, or at least I tried to pass the ball to him, but it went in the basket. The crowd went wild. I overheard the referee say, "When the going gets tough, the tough get going." Hearing this felt like a vote of confidence. It made me feel like I could do anything on the court. I heard something positive and I used that to fuel my thought process. I never forgot what that referee said, and it always reminded me that I could get the job done no matter what.

TRUST YOURSELF

What does "self" have to do with believing in oneself? Self to me means how a person sees him- or herself without all the frills. Who do you see each day when you see yourself in the mirror? Is it someone you like and are pleased with? The dictionary defines self as "one's own person apart from all other persons." Your self is you. Who you are can only be summed up as to what you are from the core.

When you are in touch with this core self, you can listen and hear more easily what is best for you. As long as you are honest with yourself, you will always make the right choices. When I graduated from high school I had scholarship offers to attend many different universities to play basketball. There were colleges that offered large sums of money. For a guy who didn't have much money, this was quite a temptation. My high school coach thought I should go to a school that had a chance to win a National Championship, and I agreed with him. Along with education, this was one of the topics we discussed when we considered colleges. I chose a college that didn't offer anything but the chance to play basketball and get an education. All things considered, I'm sure I made the right choice. I listened to my inner voice and did what felt right. I've never looked back, only forward. We never won a National Championship, but we did win the National Invitational Tournament in New York City during my junior year. I got a great **53** education and met some wonderful people who are still friends today. If I think about the other offers, I realize that I passed up a lot of money; but if I hadn't gone to Maryland, I might never have found the path that led me to Nike, to my family, and to all the other things I have today.

Even if you've made some bad choices, as long as you are honest with yourself it's never too late to turn the ship around. You are the only one who really knows who you are inside and out. Listen to yourself and do what is best for you. Never stop listening to the possibility of life. Don't stop looking into the sky and saying there is so much possible out there. If someone can launch a spaceship into orbit and land in another galaxy, you have to know that there is so much more that's possible within you. No one gets to where they are just by merely doing. They have to start believing in something and then planning and then doing. Just know within yourself that it's possible. Could I drive a Porsche or Ferrari one day? It's possible!

BELIEVE IN YOURSELF

We all are who we are.

I am who I am just as anyone else is who he or she is. I don't rob from other people's heritage but I draw strongly on mine. The only reason I put this subject in the book is because some young people have been made to feel ashamed of who they are. Particularly young people of color—who, as the descendents of slaves, sometimes feel ashamed and insignificant.

This book isn't about the color of anyone; it is about everyone feeling good about oneself. Let no one rob from you who you are. Accept who you are; there is nothing more important than being yourself. None of us had a choice in our racial design. Don't let being black or white or orange or gray hold you back. Draw your strength from those who have gone before you. Be a witness to their strength and courage. Blacks are the descendants of kings and queens from the motherland; our people were Pharaohs, scribes, and builders of the monuments of ancient Egypt. Successful people of all cultures are too numerous to list. I'm sure you have many heroes to look up to. These people didn't have it easy in their struggles to reach the top rungs of the ladder. What their tales should tell you is that it was difficult, but it can be done.

Identify whatever it is that gives you strength and follow that vision to the ends of the universe. Be strong in who you are and be diligent in your quest. You don't have to look to history to find a hero. You can look to people in your school, to the mail carrier, or to people in your community who are doing the right things. You don't have to be some big star in the minds of others to be a big star in life. Just live your life in a positive way and be an example for others to follow. Being a person of color or being white is not an excuse to not put your best foot forward. Being poor or rich is not an excuse either. You are who and what you are, and you need to work from there.

Imagine the reaction I would get if I told someone who was homeless that there was a background check done on him and he wasn't the person he thought he was. It had been discovered that he was taken away at birth from his parents who were people of royal descent. In other words, he wasn't the person that he thought he was; he was royalty. I bet that person's entire perception of himself would change. The person would probably stand taller and start to think of himself as someone special and someone who had great potential. In the same manner, the person would probably look at himself differently and, therefore, behave differently.

Now bear with me for just a second, because I'm going to skip to something heavy: It is stated in the Bible that we are all children of the Most High. This means that we are all children of God, which means that we are all princes and princesses. We are *all* of royal descent. It's just that we don't see ourselves in that light, nor do we carry ourselves in that manner.

Why shouldn't you be royalty? You have a divine right to have all the best things in life. If you shouldn't see yourself like this, who should? All the good things are waiting for you if you simply change the way you see yourself. What's holding you back? It's easy to say that this is a fairy tale and not how things work. Well, you'll never know if you aren't disposed to thinking this way. When Dr. Leedy told me I was the second most gifted person that she'd ever seen, should I have disputed her or chosen to see myself in that light? I choose to see myself in that light. You should see yourself in that light as well!

After the "Dream Team" won the 1992 Olympics, Charles Barkley was in his best shape ever. He was playing with all the superstars in the NBA. He played with the likes of Michael Jordan, Larry Bird, Magic Johnson, David Robinson, John Stockton, Chris Mullin, Scottie Pippen, and Karl Malone. We traveled to Japan right after the Olympics, and Charles was playing like I'd never seen him play. His confidence was sky high; it lasted the entire season, and he believed that he was the best in the league. That season he became the MVP (Most Valuable Player) of the NBA. His team went to the finals of the NBA Championship and he played very well. Believe you can fly, and do whatever it takes to make your dreams come true. Are you willing to work hard enough for this to become a reality? Some people are willing, while others think that it will just fall into their laps with no work at all. The latter is very risky, but if you're reading this book, I'm betting on you.

And-I Lesson

Life is meant to be lived to its fullest. From this day forward, see yourself as someone special and someone who possesses special powers and great strength. If you see yourself as a child of a higher being, you will never have anything to fear, and you will develop much more strength, wisdom, and courage—the courage and strength to face any problem head-on and win!

When no one cheers for you, cheer for yourself. You can be your own best cheerleader in life. When you fall, don't be ashamed; just get up and brush yourself off. It's OK to fall or to fail; just get up and start over again. Mrs. Bolling kept me back in the second grade. That wasn't the end of anything; it was only the beginning. I just got to start over with Mrs. Vaughn. Like MJ says with the title of his book, "I can't accept not trying." So, strike up the band!

57

The Learned Student

★

AN AND-I WARRIOR

1. *Has vision;*
2. *Sets goals;*
3. *Does what needs to be done;*
4. *Knows how to treat people;*
5. *Is part of the solution;*
6. *Has inner strength and achieves "in spite of";*
7. *Embraces change;*
8. *Listens to and learns from mentors;*
9. *Knows the rules; and*
10. *Believes in him- or herself.*

I am an And-I Warrior

IF BUT ONLY ONE

If but only one will do
Then I promise one plus one is two.
If but one can only see the light
Then somewhere along the path others will join the fight.
If but one can see the right of way
Then I know tomorrow will be a brighter day.
If I am able to be much more
Some unknown stranger will open a closed door.
If against the odds I'm able to succeed
Will I enlighten one more with this blessed deed?
For I know if but only one will believe,
And if that only one be you,
Then I know that a dream can come true,
Just as sure as the sky is blue.

I know that a head will be held high,
A spirit lifted, if you only but try.
For if that someone is you
I know your every desire will come true.
If you don't mind the bumps, scrapes, or falls,
And in spite of these things you stand tall,
I know with your mind, you'll climb any wall.
For if one can see a ray of sunlight on a cloudy day
Follow it, for it will lead the way.
If but one believes and that someone is you
I know all your hopes and dreams will come true!

THERE IS NO END

61

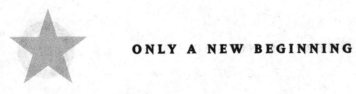

ONLY A NEW BEGINNING

The Foundation

★

HAVE I THOUGHT OF
WHO I AM TODAY?

I am And-I,
A Warrior of yesterday, tomorrow,
today, and forever.
And-I am one with the universe.
How does a bird fly?
What makes a flower bloom?
Have you seen a rainbow's signature across the sky?
Have you seen a newborn baby cry?
Do you feel me?
Do you see me in the sea?
I am And-I.
I am you and I am thee!

63

The
Master

BOOK TWO

The Inner Handbook

MY EARLY YEARS

Growing up in Hampton, Virginia, in the 1950s was quite an experience. Those days, you had to actually go out to a tree and get the switch that your parents used to beat you with. And if it was too small, your parents would get one that made you wish you had gotten a bigger switch the first time. The small ones had a lot of whip in them. In some cases, they'd hurt the worst because they would almost wrap around you.

Some children today find it hard going to school because their classmates carry guns and knives, and gangs can kill you. Fortunately, my childhood did not consist of these kinds of worries—though we did sometimes get beat up after school and I witnessed many fights. I remember that Larry Blackley, who was a bad boy in elementary school, wanted to show who was king when this new boy named Van Lewis came to school. They got into it one day when we were on our way home. Van picked up a stick and then tossed it away because he knew it would be the first thing Larry would reach for. After he threw the stick away, they started to fight. Boy, Larry got a good whipping that day. Van tore him up. Ironically, they became friends after that! But today, shooting and killing have replaced fist fighting, and kids never get to know if they could have or would have ever been friends.

We were the products of outhouses (our word for outdoor toilets), wash basins, and foot tubs for bathing. The baths usually came on Saturday nights. The rest of the time you would wash up in the basin. The water was heated on the stove, which was usually wood and coal burning—and also the source of heat for the home. This was just the reality of our lives; we didn't know there could be any other way. You see, we had our share of difficulties, but there was beauty too. I remember that I planted irises outside of the outhouse. They had the greatest smell to them, and they were a radiant purple. I watched them grow and took such pride in how they blossomed. Every time I see irises, I remember those days.

Life was a little simpler then. We didn't have computer games; we mainly had each other to play with. I loved to roller skate on the sidewalk in front of the house. Now, the best feeling in the world was skating on a newly paved road. It seemed like I could fly. We played all kinds of games—hide-and-seek, tag, and similar games. We were pretty close in the old neighborhood. When I was young, I thought it would look cool if I smoked. I would pick up cigarette butts, sneak off, light them, and smoke them. I thought I was so cool! Little did I know how ridiculous I must have seemed.

It was nice having older sisters and brothers to look up to who guided the way for me. I was the youngest in the family, so I guess I got away with a lot—but not everything. I do remember one day I was supposed to go see the Shaggy Dog movie after school and I was filled with excitement. That morning, my brother Tommy would not stop teasing me, so I got a knife and chased him upstairs. Moms caught us and that was the end of the Shaggy Dog movie. I was grounded and my show was canceled. That was the last time I tried that little trick.

I actually started playing ball late, so not everything I did was sports oriented. I led a pretty normal life. I went to the Girls and Boys Club with all the guys; we just did regular things and had fun. I never really liked baseball—it was just too slow. I would stand there and daydream. I'd play because that was what the guys wanted to do. If you're one of the guys, you have to do some of the things they want to do, so I did. I liked playing Ping-Pong. And Cowboys and Indians was a favorite of mine. I always wanted to be the chief.

We would go crabbing all the time with Moms or Sis Bertie, my mother's sister. Sometimes Aunt Nell would take us with her. (She was one of the older ladies on our street, and we all referred to her as Aunt Nell.) When they built the new bridge, they turned the old bridge into a pier, and you could fish or crab from it. The only times we ever went down to the bridge were with the older ladies in the community. Even after we became old enough to go on our own, it wasn't as much fun if the ladies weren't with us. Their influence had much to do with the people we've become.

69

It came from listening to their stories or just knowing that they cared about us.

This was a time of great love. Everyone looked out for everyone else. All the children's parents would look out for all of us. We would visit a friend and feel just as much at home as we did in our own house. We may have been poor, but I just wasn't aware of it. And if one doesn't know what poor feels like, I guess it might feel the same as rich.

When I grew up, I was just your average child. An article about me appeared in the local newspaper later, and one of the ladies down the street said, "You mean that's Howard, the little snotty-nosed kid that used to live down the street?" Yes, I guess that was me, and I'm still that same little boy. Now I just have some tissues. I grew up and matured because of all of those people, and I really thank them for what they meant in my development. I took full advantage of my childhood. It shaped my world and made me grow as a person. And I learned to take pleasure in the small things in life. I still believe that if you pay attention to all the small things, the big things will take care of themselves.

Everything I learned then I still carry with me, and I share it with others who may not have learned it yet. I guess it never really stops; it just starts all over. There is no end and there is no beginning. So, give each day your all and make it count. That is the assurance of tomorrow.

You are the rainbow of hope.
You are our bright tomorrows.
You are the future of the world.

Keep your heart pure, for that is where it all starts.
You are the purity of hope eternal.

Book 2: The Master is a compilation of stories and philosophies about life and change. They are for those readers who have tested the principles discussed in Book 1 and are ready to go deeper, to continue the transformation from apprentice to master as they work to become And-I Warriors.

The principles set forth in Book 2 are derived from years of practice and teachings; they make me who I am today. They provide a compass anyone can follow to reach his or her dreams, though this is in no way meant to suggest that everyone must do things the way I have. There is no easy method for change, but I believe that simply using these princi-ples will cause certain metamorphoses to occur. This book may open your eyes to different perspectives on spiritual awareness, the power of your mind, and your connection to others. Living by these principles, you will join the ranks of And-I Warriors, giving you the weapons for positive change for yourself and others who show the way. Learn them at your own pace. This is a chart to guide you on your journey.

TWO WORLDS

Are there two worlds? Now, I know you think I've lost my mind. I'm too far out there—*He's talking about the existence of two worlds!* The two worlds I'm talking about are the outer and inner world. There is a physical plane, which we live in everyday. And there is the inner world, which is a different one altogether.

The inner world is the place you find when you sit alone and listen to music, when late at night it's just you. Maybe you've had a few problems that day and there is no one to talk to but yourself. You just sit there with the lights out and think, What in the world have I gotten myself into? What direction should I take when facing these problems? This is you. You can't lie to yourself. This is the self that is naked before the world. This is you in the inner world, the world of feeling, prayer, and spirit where things happen that are unexplained. This is the world of emotions and hunches and intuition, the world that makes coincidence happen. Why did this happen to me? How could something like this have happened?

Now I'll tell you a story about my sister and me. This was in 1985 or '86. We were coming back from our hometown of Hampton, Virginia. I had just gotten a new car and we were making the drive back to Maryland. Truth be known, I was speeding along I-95. There were about three other cars on the freeway keeping up with me. All of a sudden I heard this noise in the engine. I told Sis that the engine was having problems. She said that she didn't hear anything and I should just keep going. "You're just hearing things; everything is fine." I knew that I heard something and I just couldn't get it out of my mind. I said I'd better pull over and check out the engine. Sis said, "I'm telling you, I don't hear anything in that engine."

Well, I pulled over and popped the hood and looked at the engine. Now, I did see a screwdriver in the little part where mechanics sometimes put their tools, but that would have been just a rattle at most. I didn't hear anything going on with the engine. Everything seemed OK. "Well, I was wrong I guess," I told Sis as I got back into the car. "It all seems fine." She said, "I told you that everything was fine." So we started back on the highway, went a little further, and then hit traffic that was backed up for miles. There must have been a terrible accident. It's just a hunch and I'll never know for sure, but I felt that the other cars that were speeding along with me were in that accident. Whatever it was, I'm glad that I had pulled over. Once we were moving again, we got off the freeway and took a back road.

That was the inner world talking to me—I'm just glad I listened. It speaks to us all. Whether we listen to it or not is a different tale. The inner world is where all things happen before they can ever become reality on the outside. This is where all the masters throughout history did their first bidding before all the great they accomplished in life. This is the start of an "A" in school and this is also the start of a "D" or an "F." This is where we put limits on ourselves or we give ourselves wings to fly. How far do you dare take yourself on your own wings? If you can't get to this world you need to go further within yourself.

Late at night or early in the morning, let your mind drift and visualize all that you want to achieve in life. See yourself as a whole new person and see what you need to reach your goal. Think of different ways available to you to accomplish your dreams. What can you do to make this thought turn into reality in the outer world? Can someone you know help you accomplish your goal? You already have the answers to all of your questions

73

inside of you. Some of us just can't get to the source to reveal the answers. When we mine gold, a lot of people give up before they ever get to the source. They settle for the gold dust (fool's gold) or the small chips they find along the way. They never make it to that big payday. They're just too impatient. Have patience. As long as you try, you will find the gold.

The outer world is the world of the physical. This is where we live and make things happen. All things that you wish for or thoughts that constantly occupy your mind manifest on this plane. You think in the inner world and it appears in the outer world. You may wish, "I want to be rich," but deep inside you think, "I'll never have enough money." And guess what? It's the deeper inner thoughts that will win. You may not even know what you have been asking for but you just keep asking over and over again. That is why you keep getting it. This may be the bad luck that just keeps following you around. Or the good. Remember, what you receive is just what you asked for.

The outer or physical world happens to be the world in which most people seek their fortunes, where you think you want those cars or that jewelry. It is where most people try to make everything happen. This is the world they think will bring them happiness. This is the world they think will give them money. This is the world they think will be there for them when all else fails. People who believe this just live day-to-day and never feel completely satisfied. How can you be happy if your happiness depends on the outer world? You don't know exactly who you are. You "become" those material things. You're them and not the real you. Not the inner you—the thinking you. So, simply *don't* let those outside things determine who you are.

Remember, if you believe enough you will get the material things you desire; the "real" world is where they must appear. But you must have balance between the two worlds. If you can't live in the world of the physical, you will certainly have some problems. If you can't live there and you live only in the inner world, you will probably be deemed crazy by those around you. You need to live in both worlds and understand the relationship between them, which can make all things come true. You must live for your dreams and your correct thoughts of your inner self. They then will materialize on the outside. Your inner self is the battlefield of the And-I Warrior!

INNER AND OUTER STRENGTH

I've spoken of the inner and outer worlds, the physical world and the spiritual world. I've said that all things we believe in the spiritual world will come to be in the world of the physical. Similarly, there are two worlds of strength. You can work out and get great physical strength. You can lift weights and become very strong and develop muscles. But the greatest strength of all is in the inner world. This is the strength that all people seek. This is that hidden strength.

When a mother can push a car off of herself and her child, she doesn't get this strength from her muscles; it's derived from a greater strength, deep inside of her. When a person is persecuted for doing nothing but right, the strength that he or she draws on is not that of the physical world but that of the inner world. In Book 1 I talked a bit about using inner strength to pursue your dreams "in spite of." It is the greatest strength you can possess. In all difficult times, this is the strength you must draw on. This is the tough part of life. But this is the part that is worth living. The important thing to remember is that you already have it inside of you; you just have to find it.

ACTIVITY

I may not be the right one to talk about this because I usually go overboard in most of the things that I do. For example, I like riding bicycles; it is a great amount of fun. I just started taking swimming lessons. I want to be a good swimmer, so I work hard at it. Before that I was always playing tennis. I would play as much as my schedule allowed.

Before that I trained our dog, Tiffany. We trained all of the time; eventually we went to dog shows and I showed her in the obedience ring. We won a CDX title, which stands for Companion Dog Excellence. Before that I played basketball. When I was small I rode stick horses and jumped rope with the girls.

The point I'm trying to make is that—regardless of what you choose—you should engage in some type of physical activity in your life. It is not necessary to go overboard as I do. I'm emphasizing the importance of doing something for your body. You only get one during your lifetime; therefore you should take care of it. Try to eat right and do things in moderation. You might do something as simple as walk—walking is good for you. You should drink at least eight glasses of water a day; we often forget that the body is made mostly of water and can easily get dehydrated. So drink plenty of water and watch what you eat. Engaging in physical activity is good. It makes for a sound body.

Likewise, don't neglect the mind. Brains need exercise just like bodies do—something active, not passive like watching TV. If you learn to enjoy something like reading, you will be a long ways down the road to having a sound mind. Reading is something you will always use, and the more you read, the better you will comprehend. And because everything starts on the inside, the things you learn end up popping up in other places. Had I paid more attention in French, the first time I went to France I would have been able to speak to the people better. But when I was in school I never thought I'd go to France. If on the inside I would have believed I would go to France, I would have gotten there faster (and I would have studied the language better). It starts on the inside.

ELEVEN

Power

★

MIND

When I was young, I thought about all kinds of things.
I lived a good amount in the world of my imagination. I thought about ways of scoring. When I saw big
machines, I thought about the power they represented and
wondered whether people could use that type of power to make
things happen. I focused on power, with the control tower being
my mind. Somewhere along the road I realized that thought is
the ultimate thing in the universe, or at least it is connected to
that which is the ultimate. It is the power that makes all things
happen, and the connection to it is what separates the weak from
the strong.

Keep in mind what Thomas Edison is quoted as saying:
"Genius is 1 percent inspiration and 99 percent perspiration."
It's true. You may want to write this down and post it where
you'll see it regularly, just to remind you of what's possible if

you stick to your goals. The mind is such a powerful tool that we don't even know how strong and powerful it is. What you must accept is that you are a part of all things. You have the power to *affect* all the things that happen to you. You must remember that you are a part of the great powers of the universe. You have the power to release them or deny them.

THOUGHT

We can't talk about the power of the mind without talking again about positive thinking. A single drop of water is harmless and can be gentle. But when it goes together with force in a tidal wave, it cannot be stopped. Thoughts are like this too.

The mind is like a garden. What you plant is what can grow. But it doesn't matter if you plant the greatest garden in the world; if you don't take care of it, it will be overrun by weeds. When that happens, you may not harvest any of the things that you planted. So, you have to weed and feed your garden with care to make sure the crop is a good one. Your mind is the same. You must put positive things in there and weed and feed them to ensure a good crop. Positive thoughts are what you must constantly put into your mind: forget *don't*, *can't*, and *if*. You need only, from this point forward, to concentrate on *can*, *do*, and *will*. Remember that you can do anything that you put your mind to.

If you don't control what goes into your mind, negative thoughts find their way in, and those will dictate the results. Because so many people struggle with feelings of lack of fulfillment, denial, low self-esteem, loss, hatred, disgust, and anger, they often end up with more of the same. You must *actively* think positive thoughts or, like dust, negative thoughts will settle. When these unwanted thoughts form in your mind, you can either control them or they will control you.

If you think positively, you will be positive. If you think negatively, you will be negative. It's a matter of perception. Not all people perceive things in the same manner. When two people look at the same thing, one might view it as bad, while the other might see it as good. How is this so when both people saw the same thing? How you choose to see a thing determines how it can affect you. If you get a bad grade you can either see it as "I'm just not that smart" or simply "I need to work harder. I can get together with the teacher and see just where I'm lacking." Once you realize that it is all part of a (81) process and that to get good at something, you need to find out where your weaknesses are, then finding out where more work is needed isn't a bad thing, it's good! Subsequently, you will commit more time and effort to the class. Do you see the glass as half empty or half full?

A friend of mine said that when she was growing up, her form of punishment was being sent to her room. She disliked her stepfather and when he made her go to her room she would read and read. She took this punishment and turned it into something positive. The books became her friends. She started to like being in her room and looked forward to spending time there. This is what life is all about. Turn something negative into something positive. Your mind is the greatest escape route in the world. Books are one of those highways you can take to escape.

Don't sit back and become miserable dancing to someone else's music. When you create your own music, you can dance the dance that you want. Be your own one-man or one-woman band. You can march to the beat of your own drummer. Take things that you hear other people say about you that are positive and hold on to them. When you hear people say negative things about you, don't dwell on them.

Once a good friend confided that one of her twins wasn't quite as sharp as the other one. The twins were fraternal—one of them was a boy and the other was a girl. She said that the girl just didn't seem to catch on to things as quickly as the little boy did. Her parents feared that she would do poorly in school and feel worthless because her brother was much smarter. After I heard that, from then on, I would talk to her and tell her she was a genius. Whenever we talked I would tell her that she must know the answer because she was a genius and surely, if she didn't know the answer, any good genius would know how to find it. I did this to give her encouragement. Eventually I moved away, but I would still call her every chance I got and tell her that she was my genius.

Guess what—she started believing that she was a genius. She began finding all the answers. Her schoolwork improved. She started going to the library to get books she needed in order to find the answers. Her mother filled me in on her progress. She studied and studied and worked and worked and became an "A" student and developed a great image of herself. If someone asked her, she wouldn't hesitate to tell them immediately that she was a genius. When she was grown up and going to college, she told her mother that her first car would sport the license plate "Genius." Today Rona has that car with the "Genius" plate and an excellent job with the CIA.

This is how the power of the mind can work. Positive thinking will make most things come true. Whatever you put into your brain and truly believe, your mind will work to make come true. The key is to make sure your mind is filled with positive images. You are who you think you are.

The first thing to do when you wake up in the morning, before you get out of bed, is to think good thoughts. Imagine yourself having a great day—successfully completing your tasks while maintaining a positive, happy attitude. Imagine yourself projecting your *positivity* out into the world. Don't be alarmed when you experience negative thoughts or worries about unpleasant things that you may have to face. Negative thoughts come to us each day. Just remind yourself of your determination to keep negative thoughts out of your mind. This is not the easiest task in the world. But you must remember that what goes in is what will show up on the outside.

Finally, let me add this to your thought process: The most important work isn't done on the outside. The real work that we need to do is on our inner self. We need to continually put in the positive thoughts and the rest will take care of itself. Remember what Mahatma Gandhi said, "Guard your beliefs because they become your thoughts. Guard your thoughts because they become your actions. Guard your actions because they become your habits. Guard your habits because they become your values. Guard

83

your values because they become your destiny." It simply starts with what you believe.

MAP TO THE ZONE OF TRUTH

If you are beginning to think that all things, both good and bad, start with the power of your thoughts, you are starting to know your real power. If you view the outside world of hate, need, suffering, pain, poverty, and injustice like a large forest that you are approaching and can't see your way through, I am giving you a map to peace of mind. Now, I want you to think of the state you're in when you're somewhere just listening to a nice, soft, relaxing song. I want you to think of the inner you that is sitting with your eyes closed and just listening to what is within you. The lights are out and all that is there is you and your thoughts—the quiet thoughts that are the real you. The true you.

No matter what you've done or not done in life, you want to forget about being down on yourself. Now you want to think in terms of the you that you really want to be. It's never too late to get started.

Let's start the walk into the forest. At first, all you see are the big trees that seem to block your path and the rough ground that is covered with pine needles and small brush. The forest is so thick with all of these trees! You can't really see where it is you're supposed to be heading. Look inward just a little deeper and you can see it. There it is: a little path—something you've never seen before in the midst of all of the trees and bushes. The path starts to wind and twist, but it isn't too hard to follow.

Just keep on the path, and now you see some flowers that have started to come into view. They are beautiful flowers, like none you've ever seen before. The colors are not like any you know. They are bright and full of life. The reds that you see are so lush; the blues are amazingly blue. Look at the oranges and the greens that pop right out at you. You want to stop, but you must keep going further and further. The smell is so fresh and alive. You can't believe the aroma that is coming from all of the beauty that is around you. Look! There is the most beautiful bird that you've ever seen. You can't really tell what kind of bird it is. You're looking at it. You know that it has a strange and beautiful hue. It flies by you, but you're not afraid. You follow it down the path as you go deeper into the forest. Your footsteps get lighter and you see clearer than you've ever seen before.

85

Your footsteps quicken and the path seems to be even more alive. You just go further and you know that this is where you want to be. There is a feeling of closeness about you. You are at peace with the world. Are you alone? Or is someone with you other than that wonderful bird that you've followed? You come upon big rocks and you must climb to get over them. You climb over them and now you're looking down a little ravine. You climb down and the path continues. There are a few bushes in front of you that you peek through, then you walk just a little further. You look down into a crystal blue lake. It is the most beautiful place you've ever seen or even dreamed of. You see, this is the center of all things. It is your center and your place of life. Here you can view the world as it just passes by. Here, you are all things and you are at one with all things. All the colors that you viewed were a compilation of you. They were all the things that you had ever envisioned.

This is the place where it all begins. This is where you see the real you. There are no tricks that you can play on yourself. There are no lies that you can use to hide from yourself. It is just you, the real you, the person you want to be all the time. The kingdom of heaven is within. The center of life is within. You're there now. You're in this kingdom and you are at one with it. You are at peace with it. Whatever it is you need to know, you know. Whatever it is you need to see, you see. Who and whatever you want to be, you are. All things that you want, you have. You have no lack, no want; there is no limitation placed on you; you are all things and all things are you. You are! If you want to take flight, you simply think it and it happens. You just lift your arms and they become wings. As you think to be, you are ... *you are!*

AND-I MEDITATION

I am a being of power. My mind is receptive. Whatever I put in it will come to be.

I will feed all parts of me with positive energy. When I need to be strong it will be there for me and give me all the strength that I need to be a whole and complete person.

In all things that happen I see the good and not the bad. I may have to try harder to see this good, but I know it is there and I will find it. I open my eyes and see.

TWELVE

Spirit

★

SPIRITUAL AWARENESS

When I was growing up, part of life was that you went to Sunday School. Then, as you got older, you went to church. That was just the way life was. No questions were asked. You just did it. I'm not quite sure when this routine turned into something else. I don't consider myself an especially religious person, but I do believe that there is something that is far greater than we are in the universe. The great thing is that we're all a part of it—it really doesn't matter what religion you practice or if you're not part of any religion.

Religion may not be for everyone, but I think that everyone can be spiritual. Spirituality can give us a certain balance and focus and make us humble. It can let us see that there is a far greater power than you and me. It can give us a certain inner strength and peace to get us through the most difficult times. It can even give insight into what life is all about. When introduced at a young age, spirituality can lay an important foundation that will serve us well as we become adults.

The phenomenal power that makes a flower bloom is within you as well. Whatever your faith, it's important to take time every day to become quiet so that you can find some inner peace and reconnect with that power. Be aware of a greater force in the world than yourself. And believe that whatever the source of this power—God or Mother Nature—it is willing to help you.

FAITH

First we must understand that faith is something unseen.

Faith plays an important part in this book; it provides the foundation on which my premise is built. The amount of belief or faith that you possess will determine how much you will receive or how far you will go in life.

Another part of faith is understanding that good things will happen for you, though your life may not always turn out exactly as you plan. When you strive for a goal that gets pulled away from your grasp, open your eyes—some higher purpose is at work. When I injured my knee in college, I had to realize that I wasn't going to become the "Big O" in the pros, but all my work in that direction wasn't wasted. The discipline and success that I experienced on the court has been useful in every part of my life since I stopped playing ball. When one door closes, another opens, and you must always have faith in that.

Most people believe or have faith in something as long as it's going their way. The trick is to remain faithful when all seems lost and everyone has turned their backs or when things look like they're not going to go your way. That is faith. Many people do not receive simply because they don't truly believe that they *will* or because they don't believe that they deserve the better things in life. "Oh, ye of such little faith"— that's what I echo to my friends when something good happens to them that they thought had little chance of happening. We all want things, but the truth is, we don't often believe that we deserve to have what we really want. The first time the path gets a little narrow or the road gets somewhat bumpy, we want to turn back. Remember my friend Rudy Garcia-Tolson? He has no legs yet he gets up each morning knowing that he can move mountains. He has to know that he has all he needs and believe in his dreams. That is the type of faith I'm talking about, the kind of faith that comes from listening to a voice deep inside yourself, and ignoring the nay-sayers. It's all inside of you and you must be able to tap into it.

89

I was talking to the boxer Roy Jones Junior. He said that his greatest moment was when he fought a championship fight and could only use one hand because he had hurt the other. He felt that something stronger had taken over that allowed him to outsmart his opponent. Once when Michael Jordan was sick and hadn't slept because he had been vomiting all night, something stronger took over and assisted him in playing his best game when his team needed him the most. The Bulls went on to win that game and subsequently their fifth world championship.

When you know what you are reaching for, you should hold it in mind at all times. Picture something perfect and beautiful.

Know that whatever it is will come if you simply believe and have faith. There are always those who have eyes and will not see and those who have ears and will not hear. But you still have the choice to be one of those who see through the darkness. When you quiet yourself and become one with the darkness, you *do* start to see. The key is to believe, every single day of your life.

PRAYER

In this mode, I will talk about prayer. Not prayer as you know it but something that may seem a little foreign to you. This is my concept of prayer. To get to this I must tell you first that the mind is made up of two parts. The first is the conscious mind, which is the mind that we think with all the time. This is our controlling force.

The second mind is the subconscious mind. This mind is the part of us that is so powerful. It is capable of creating and accomplishing everything that we want. What's tough is getting the good stuff in there so that this subconscious mind can go to work for us—or, rather, start making things happen that are the good things that we want. Now follow me on this! If we ask a man who was abused as a child to comment on abuse, he will tell us that abuse is the worst thing in the world. He may even go so far as to tell us that, when he has children, he will treat them much better. What is amazing is that when many such people have children, they repeat the exact same behavior toward their children that they experienced. They will abuse their own kids just as they were abused, although in their conscious mind they will tell you that they would never want to do that. The subconscious mind has remembered what was done to them. What is deep down inside of them works to make that happen again in their adult life. Most of the time these people need counseling to change their behavior so they can deal with what's deep inside themselves.

You must keep putting good things into your mind so those good things will happen in your life. It has been proven that there is one thing in life that never stops. It never sleeps and it is always ongoing. It works 365, 24/7. (For you older readers, that is 365 days a year and 24 hours a day, 7 days a week.) It never stops—your subconscious mind is always on the job!

I believe that prayer is just the process of thinking good thoughts always. They will get into your subconscious mind. Good things will always come in, and good things will always happen to you. Period! Try starting out each day with a little prayer. It doesn't have to be long—just something to wake up the spirit inside and give a little thanks. Then take just a little quiet time each night as well to reflect on the day's events. Take time to sum up what you've accomplished—just something to give the mind a rest from all of the happenings of the day.

What I'm trying to convey through this book is that thought is prayer, and whatever you think sooner or later comes into your world or reality. I've mentioned this again because I don't want you to live at the mercy of negative thoughts. If your early years weren't a good experience, you can start over today and repro-gram your mind. All of us have been conditioned from birth. What we've seen and heard has become our reality. It has been said that we are all born butterflies, and by age six we've begun putting ourselves back into the cocoon. I want you to realize that if life hasn't been that wonderful for you and you've had a rough time of growing up, you possess the power and knowledge to make a change within yourself. Understand that change is continuous. You are not destined to be a certain way forever just because that is how you are today. No matter what type of life you've had, today is the beginning of your transformation! Your journey will begin with the simple process of prayer or the way you start thinking about all things. This process won't be an overnight change, especially if you have been living with the same unhappy thoughts all your life. Now you have a different way to think about all things in your life and make a change for the better. Prayer is getting the good thoughts into your precious subconscious. So, I want you to keep putting positive thoughts into your mind. Remember, the more you put in, the better the chance you have for it to reach the real source. Keep the process alive—*especially* when things seem like they're going wrong—and it will make a difference in your life.

You have to believe in something, and whatever it is I hope it's something that's good and decent. Remember that whatever you believe in is what you will be praying to 24/7. Your subconscious is always active—even as you sleep. My belief is that whatever you think of deeply enough goes right into your subconscious process and radiates into the universe. This is what comes back to you. You believe in what you ask for and to practice what you preach. Since you're in control of what you put into this machine, you are the only one who will have to take responsibility for who you become.

Let me digress for a minute and talk about something else. This matter can be summed up with the spirit of one person who comes to mind. The inner strength that I am talking about is what Nelson Mandela showed the world when he was in prison. He was jailed in South Africa. He was put into solitary confinement for the first seven years and was not allowed to touch his wife. After the first seven years he still wasn't allowed any type of communication. He couldn't read a newspaper, watch television, nor listen to a radio. When he was released from prison after twenty-seven years, he wasn't angry or upset. He said that he didn't have time for such things. After his release, he led a nation out of bondage. He became the president of South Africa, a leader to the same people who had put him in jail. What do you think kept him going all of that time? It had to be prayer. It was the strength of his mind and his inner strength. His thoughts and his faith were all he had. This is what real strength is, and we all must strive for it. At seventy-three, Nelson Mandela became the president of South Africa after being in jail for twenty-seven years. This is what the power of prayer and faith can do for you. Belief can start with something as simple as the power of thought.

93

AND-I MEDITATION

I am much more than I give myself credit for being. I believe that I am given strength through a higher power and it will guide and direct my every step along the path. This strength rests deep within me. *The power of a higher being rests within me. This source of contentment is mine.*

I will be strong in my beliefs and convictions.

I use my path to that place that is most special that lies within me. I go there when all around me in the outer world gets to be too much for me to handle. The more I go there, the stronger I become. I know that as it is within me, one day it will be likewise in the outside world.

There is an endless supply of faith from which I can draw. It is there for not only me but for all who come to be replenished. My cup truly does run over.

You are God's gift to us
You are a seed of goodness
And of hope

Do not fear

Speak your truth
But listen to the counsel of spiritual friends

Do not fear

Walk alone in your truth if you must
Keep the vision
Remember you are also a dream
You are our hope
Our deeper longings for love

Speak what you feel
But remember compassion

Make the music you play
And the songs you sing
A gift to those who sing
To those who have lost the gift of song
And to those who dance and to those
Who no longer hear the music

Do not fear your desires
Know that your desires are but cravings
For those things that the world finds important

Understand the greater craving
For things that are beyond this world

Still live each moment as the miracle that it is
Allow your passions to consume you

Allow your inner love to guide you
Your heart to lead you
Your mind to know the way

Never concede to confusion
Admit it: there are some things you know
Some things that you do not know
And some things that you cannot know

Make circumstance an opportunity for self-expression
This is the secret of the journey

It is the constant struggle between
How we would like to be seen by others
How we see ourselves
And how we are seen through the eyes
Of the Beloved

Do not fear

Your nature is Divine
You are a sacred flame
In a sacred Fire
Lit by God

You are
And-I
Am
The keeper of the flame

Go forth Pilgrim of Light
Discover within yourself

The Great Beloved

—Thomas M. White

THIRTEEN

Love

This is the universal code word. Everyone in the world wants love. As with respect, to get love you must first have a great deal of love for yourself. Love yourself completely and honestly. You'll find out that the more you're capable of loving and sending love out into the world, the stronger you'll become in your growth. You'll find that if you love, many good things will happen for and to you. It can be challenging to love those who you feel don't like or care for you or those whom you have difficulty liking. But these are the people who need your love in the worst way. It takes too much energy to hate and to do spiteful things out of hurt that only come back to you a negative way anyway. Hate is not the answer to any of the world's problems.

If someone doesn't care for you, I'm not saying you should run up to them every day and profess your love for them. What I'm saying is that you must feel love for them within your heart and move forward. In effect, when you send love out into the

97

universe, the spirit of love and goodwill will come back to you. Love is the single most effective tool in the universe for making a difference in your life. What is it that they say? God is love! Have a love for all things—trees, plants, animals, people. In these things, see love. See the importance in them and you will see the importance in yourself. When you do this you stop being just someone who is a target for anything that happens. You will begin to be a special creature of the universe. I call it being a child of the universe. Through love you will become at one with all things and all things will be at one with, or be a part of, you.

Love comes in many forms. Don't make the mistake of thinking that love is the same as sex. That is the only form of love for which some people have any frame of reference. They have not experienced other love while growing up. The only love they know is the kind they learned in the outside world—physical love. Real love is something deeper, and goes further than something between just two people. It connects us with everything in the universe.

FRIENDS

I have many friends and they are all great people. They have come into my life and taught me many things. If you start living the principles in this book (such as having a positive outlook on all things), you'll find that people come into your life for a reason. They may be there to teach you things or you may be one of their teachers. You should try to surround yourself with positive people. Look for friends who are trying to make positive things happen in their lives. Some people look at roses and see only the thorns, and some look at them and see a wonderful flower protected by the thorns. People who are upbeat are a joy to be around, while those who always choose to see the worst side of life tend to be a drag—like a ball and chain around your neck. This principle is linked to *your* attitude and to the way *you* think.

You're going to learn from those people with whom you come in contact, so make them good, solid people. Having great friends is easy, because this is something that, once again, you get to choose. Just make good choices. I know many of you will say you don't get to choose your friends; they're just there. But I say that you know the difference between right and wrong. All of the people you come in contact with won't be your peers, nor do you want them to be. But they can be good people and have good values. If people are stealing or telling lies to make themselves look good, you don't have to be in their company.

Phil Knight may be the chairman and CEO of Nike, Inc., but more importantly he is my friend. Our friendship has changed my understanding of the world, professionally and personally. It's funny how opportunities come into your life. Are they merely coincidence, or are you *making* them happen?

The suggestions in this book really do work if you believe in and work at them. Once you start to think good, "right," positive thoughts, the people who will become your friends are the people whom your thoughts will bring into your world. It goes back to the way you think. If your thoughts are positive and pure, so too are the people you attract; and if your thoughts are negative, you attract negative people. I know it sounds simple but it does work. Like attracts like. Be cautious in your selection of friends.

HAPPINESS

Happiness is far too important to leave up to anyone else. I've heard from so many people that they just can't seem to be happy, and everyone they come in contact with fails to make them happy. Heed these words: I make *myself* happy!

This is another of those important things for which you can take control. In everything you see, focus on the good. Remember this! The thorns of the brier patch are inevitable, but there is always another way to look at what happens in life. If it's raining, think of how beautiful and green the grass will be because of it. Think how wonderful it is when you hear the singing of birds. Appreciate the beautiful things around you. The world is full of beauty. Learn to love the smaller things. Take a walk in the early morning and smell the freshness of the new day. Watch a sunset or a sunrise. Watch little children at play. See yourself in all of these scenes and think about happiness. The longer you do this, the more in tune you become with your own happiness. Your moods won't shift like a blade of grass in a windstorm. If something bothers you, look for the beauty and wonder in your surroundings. It may be a butterfly or a flower. It may be the snow falling or the rain dancing on the window-sill. You can find happiness in any movement, no matter what is happening around you. You make yourself happy. Don't leave it up to anyone else.

FORGIVENESS

Forgiveness is a universal law. You can't think good positive thoughts if, on the inside, you harbor ill feelings toward other people. As I've said, if someone does something to you that you think is bad or wrong, the truth is that they haven't done anything to you but only to themselves.

Let me also say again that I truly believe that all the people who come into my life are there for a reason. Each one teaches me a great deal about who I am and where I'm going in life. In college, one of the guys on the basketball team that I coached started secretly dating my fiancée. Of course, as life would have it, I was the last to know. When I found out about the two of them, I spoke to them both. She and I continued dating, then later broke off the engagement. John and I drifted apart—for a time.

John had been a star in college and went on to become the number-one player picked in the basketball draft during his senior year. John lived the good life a little too much in school and in the pros. He ran into some bad luck, turned down the wrong street in life, and started using drugs. He started missing games and not taking trips with his team. When I saw this I thought to myself, "He needs to be around some good people." He needed a true friend, and I became one. We started hanging out and doing things together. As it turned out, John became my connection to Nike. His sister was dating Nike's East Coast basketball representative, who was moving out west. John told me about the job that would be available in the area. I didn't know this person, but I looked him up in the phone book one day and called him, and we got together a few times. He told me to send him a résumé, which I did. One day, out of the clear blue sky—maybe six months after we had met—he called me and said the job was mine; when could I start working? It was quite a shock.

From out of nowhere, this job came into my life. Many guys whom I know (and possibly some that you know), might have felt good when John got into trouble. They might have thought, "Oh well, the guy is just getting what he deserves." But remember, no one does anything to anyone else—they only do it to themselves. If I'd chosen to turn my back on John out of my own hurt, I would have only hurt myself and added to the misery in the world. Instead I reached out to help a fellow human with forgiveness at the forefront of my mind, and if I hadn't done so I wouldn't have the life I have now. Paying attention to experiences like this has taught me that more good will always come if you start from a foundation of love and forgiveness. We should all use this principle, for it is powerful and it does work. You must forgive; your anger only hurts you.

AND-I MEDITATION

I strive to remember that love is the most powerful tool in the universe. Those who are the most difficult to love are those who need it the most. I surround myself with positive people so we can lovingly support each other.

I know that I am my own source of happiness. I can't make anyone else happy if I'm not truly happy myself.

I forgive those who I feel have wronged me. Keeping negative thoughts inside only clouds my mind and prevents the good from finding me. There is so much good waiting to happen to me, and I don't let anything get in its way! I deserve everything that is mine.

FOURTEEN

Passion

★

Whenever possible, try to do things with passion. It doesn't matter if it's your schoolwork or your hobby or the work that you do to provide for yourself. If you have to do something anyway, it really doesn't take that much more of an effort to go all out. You can do things halfheartedly, without making any real commitment, but you must expect that your results will be the same as the effort that you put into the process. It's all about the way you approach things.

When I attempt something, I always think of the greatest people that have previously done what I'm undertaking. As I said earlier, I love to ride bicycles, and I ride them with passion. I think of myself as being Miguel Indurain, five-time winner of the Tour de France—he was the best in the sport at that time. I also think of April Holmes, who won a gold medal at the Paralympics. She didn't feel sorry for herself after she lost her leg. When I played basketball I thought of being the "Big O," the best of his day. When I played tennis I thought of being John McEnroe. If you want to be the best, just think of the best people who have done what you're attempting to do.

If it's music that makes you happy, think of the people who are the best performers. You can't think of being the best if you aren't willing to research what others have done and know how much time and effort they've put into being the best. No one just starts out being the best—they must work at it continuously.

The special people I know aren't really any different from anyone else until they do what it is that makes them special. Great piano players, writers, or professors don't know how special they are until they approach their craft. They may not do many other things particularly well; sometimes they even perform other things particularly badly. But when it comes to what they do well, they perform like nobody's business. Extraordinary people are simply ordinary people who are on fire with desire. So if you want to be extraordinary, get excited about life and go for it with all your heart and soul. If you give life everything you have, you will feel wonderful about your effort and your achievement.

YOUR GIFT

Each of us has a special gift. Sometimes people grow up knowing exactly what they want to do or be, but more often it takes work to find out. Either way, this gift is somewhere inside you, waiting to unfold. You may already feel it or it may be buried deep inside of you, but it is there.

Now, there are a lot of presents just sitting there that will never get the chance to be opened. Too many people don't take the time to be still long enough to see what this gift is that they possess. They are too busy with the world around them to find out what is trying to unfold within them. Learning how to get there is a valuable lesson.

You are a being who is capable of great things. You are a special person who was brought here for a special reason. You have a great gift inside of you. Deep inside of you is the power of all that has ever happened and all that can ever happen! Too many of us never connect with this awesome power. Few of us have the focused power to open the door and reach inside to bring out the best in ourselves. What holds this door shut is one thing and one thing only: fear! We all have within us something that we can do as well as or better than anyone in the world. The trick is finding out what that something is. Most great things that happen take long periods of time. The Egyptian pyramids were not built overnight. Your job is figuring out what's most important to you and then pursuing it.

Try to be aware of all the things around you and all the things that you do. There are some things you really enjoy doing or that you may be particularly good at. You may be able to run a little faster than others. Math may come a little easier to you than it does for your classmates. You may be the class clown, able to hold everyone's attention. You may have a gift for numbers or spelling or vocabulary, or caring for people or animals. You may be the one who people feel they can go to for help, someone who people listen to. Start being aware of all things around you and listen to what your teachers tell you, in school or just in life. Apply selective listening to choose the advice that can make your life better; in other words, listen for compliments on your abilities and tune out people who tell you negative things. Finding your talent may not be easy. Sometimes you may not see the gift at first. Trust that the river of life knows where it's going and know that you'll be okay.

Do not spend time dwelling on the past, and don't put all of your effort into thinking of the future. The past is just that: past. You can't change it, but you can learn from it. You can't spend all of your time worrying about it. The future is where you want to be. Now hear me loud and clear: I'm *not* telling you not to prepare for the future, for it will be here sooner than you think! I *am* telling you there is nothing that will take the place of the precious *now*, the present. For it is the now in which all great things happen. The now is the time to get things done; don't put them off until some other time. My mother's generation would say, "Don't put off until tomorrow what you can do today." That way it's done and you can move on. People spend too much time worrying about things that never happen or brooding about things that will never change because there is nothing on this earth they can do about them.

The moment of truth is now. Relax; be still and silent to find the precious gift that is yours alone. There is something that awaits you. I hope that the two of you find each other, that you and your gift meet and become one with each other.

My gift is related to people. I feel people make the world go around, and my life is one of service to them. We get money because we provide a service to people: we don't get because we take; we get because we give. And the more you give, the more you'll get back. People who are successful usually feel they have provided something that the rest of the world can't do quite as well as they can. Be of service to people. Bill Gates hasn't done too badly with software. Neither did Alexander Graham Bell with the telephone.

Some people see a straight road to their heart's desire. Others must follow a less direct path. But in either case, everything you learn on the way will come in handy at some point. No knowledge gained is ever wasted. I've grown as a businessperson from all the lessons I've learned throughout my career. My coaching experience at the University of Maryland was very important, as well as my running the intramural department; even my short experience in the insurance industry has paid off. So even if you're doing a job you don't like, try to get the most that you can out of it, since you never know how that experience will help you down the road.

If you want to be good at something, do what other people aren't willing to do. If it takes getting up at four in the morning to prepare for an examination or presentation, do it. Take the initiative. Even with something as simple as taking out the trash, there is a way to turn it into something special. You should wash out the trash can a few times a month; you should never have to be told to do it. Just do it with pride and energy. Don't be one of those people who have to be told every little thing and do a halfhearted job at whatever it is they are doing. Whether it is the lowest job in the world or the most glamorous, you can do it with dignity. For every job was once lowly, until someone made people recognize the importance of the job and the person doing it. If no one sees what a good job you are doing, it's still good to practice this attitude, because then working hard will become a habit. And eventually it will be noticed.

After college, my good friend Ron Council said that people should get all of the degrees that they can. I told him that it must be the thing he should do, and he did it; he earned his Ph.D. Now he is Dr. Council. I told Ron that my future rested with people—I had always felt that interacting with people was my strong suit. For as long as I can remember, people have followed me; whether it was on a stick horse or a basketball court or just in life, I've loved people. I told Ron his thing was getting all of the education he needed, and I would take care of knowing all of the people that we both needed. So, if he needs something that involves people he will call me, and if it's something that involves the books, I'll call him. It seems like a pretty good trade-off to me.

I have a knack for helping people discover their gifts. Sometimes all we need is a helping hand to pull the bow that wraps the present. All some people need is a little encouragement to see that they too have a wonderful gift inside of them, waiting to be released. People all along my path have shown me my gifts. Do I not owe others the pleasure of helping them find their ribbons in life? Look for your gifts and help others find theirs too. Don't be one of those who never finds his or her purpose or who stands by and watches someone else's great potential go to waste. If you find the bow that wraps your gift, you will find within the treasures of a lifetime. Seek with all diligence, for the answer is there. A hope for the best possible tomorrow lies within you today.

AND-I MEDITATION

Sitting quiet and still, I look deep inside and discover my true passion.

I take note of my gifts and strive to improve them, using the example of others who have gone before me. Along the way, I give encouragement to others.

I tackle all tasks with my best effort.

FIFTEEN

Honor

Sometimes you're ahead,
sometimes you're behind.
The race is long,
And, in the end,
it's only with yourself.

—Mary Schmich

Honor is something that no amount of fame and fortune can buy. But it can be sold, and once it is sold you have it no more. If you have confidence and integrity, honor will surely be yours; they are interlocking pieces of the puzzle.

One definition of integrity is the state of being complete or undivided; this is what you should strive for. You should have such confidence in your person that you never hold your head anywhere but high. Not money, nor the way you look or dress, nor how you comb or part your hair can give you any of these treasures; only the thoughts you hold and the way you live your life. My niece, Lisa White Fairfax, told me that she decided at Moms's funeral she would have no regrets in her life. When you live your life with honor, there is no reason for regret.

I've known people of power, fortune, and fame who lacked honor. Sooner or later, when they get found out, they want to run and hide and their confidence runs and hides with them. If you have honor you will be able to face any problem that comes your way. You will stand your ground and fight any fight with confidence and the shield of integrity, for you will be the master of the situation and you will be on the side of right. Keep confidence and integrity, and you will always have a solid and firm ground on which to stand tall.

HONESTY

There is only one someone in life with whom you must be honest, and that someone is you! Being honest is your passport to success.

When you are dishonest with yourself, the only one who loses is you. You're probably thinking that a lot of people do get ahead by cheating or cutting corners. This may be true, but somewhere down the road it catches up to them. Deep inside, they have to live with themselves, knowing that they've done wrong.

The times I tried to get ahead by cheating or being dishonest, I ended up worse off than when I started. It doesn't matter whether someone else catches you. The person who gets or doesn't get the benefit of your actions will ultimately be you.

Cheat if you'd like, lie or steal if you'd like, but the only one you are hurting is y-o-u, that is, *yourself*. It is one of those crazy laws of the universe.

You must understand that this concept—that you get what you ultimately deserve because of your actions—is not *sometimes* true; it is 100 percent true *all* of the time, 365 days a year. It's the circle again. We reap what we sow, and what you do does come back to you. Now, here is the hardest part of that equation: you don't get to pick when it comes back. It may be the worst possible time of your life for something bad to happen to you. Remember this, for it is not just sometimes true but it is always true—always!

Don't put on airs or try to be someone or something that you're not. If you're a phony, others will see through you sooner or later. People will see right through your cover and they will blow it for you. If you learn only one thing from this book, I hope it is that *you're important*. If you have a hard time believing it, follow the ideas that I talk about in here and you will increasingly believe it. You'll take pride in the person that you're becoming. I hope you don't want to be anyone else but who you are. We all think it is easier to walk in someone else's shoes than it is to walk in our own. Trust me on this one—it just *looks* easier. We don't know how difficult life is for others until we've walked a mile in their shoes. People of fame and fortune don't necessarily have it easy because they're famous. You have the best shoes for you. You're the only you there is. Take pride in this and look for your special gift that you can provide to the world. If you are honest with yourself, and see your true self, you will start being honest with the world—and you will only strive to be you. Be sincere and forthright and it will pay off when it is most needed.

I grew up in an environment of honesty. Well, unless telling the insurance man that Moms wasn't home qualifies as dishonest. But we were supposed to tell the truth.

Once when I was in high school, I went into a supermarket to get some candy. When I got to the cash register the lady asked me if that was all I wanted. I said, "Yes."

She asked me, "Are you sure?"

I said, "Yes."

She said, "What about what you have in your pocket?"

I said I didn't have anything in my pocket. I had to pull my pocket inside out to show her. Maybe she actually thought she'd seen me take something, but I felt that she only asked this because I was a black kid—or just because I was a kid, period—and she felt the reason I was in the store was to steal. That was just her opinion of me. But when you're honest and you have to prove who you are, so be it. Maybe this changed her opinion of the other black kids or kids in general who walked into the store. It didn't change the opinion I had toward other people or make me think that others had it out for me. I could have gotten upset and decided that all white people thought black children, or maybe all children, were dishonest. Or I could let it serve as an opportunity to show another quality: honesty.

People can think what they want, but it's up to you whether your accusers will be right or not. Again, this puts only you in control of your own destiny. It was painful to be questioned in front of the other customers. I was embarrassed. My integrity had been questioned! I wanted to share this story with you so you'd realize that you and I aren't so different. I'm sure that someone has accused you of doing something that you didn't do or not given you the benefit of being someone of honest character. I want you to remember that when you are accused, this just gives you a platform to show your true colors. You always have control over one thing: you. You always have control over your actions and reactions to any situation in life.

LEADERSHIP

The future of the world is up to the leaders and those who choose to follow them. Ninety percent of the people in the world are looking for someone to follow. The other 10 percent are leaders. Now, of that 10 percent you'll have half who lead for the good and right causes in life and half who lead for the other side. These leaders for the bad are just as effective as those who lead for the good, and the bad way may often seem an easier route to take. If you are one of the 90 percent, I hope you choose your leaders well.

If you're one of those who can lead, I hope you take care of your followers and make a good effort at what you must do. There are ways to make things happen that don't include guns and knives and bullets and clubs. Look at leaders like Jesus, Gandhi, and Martin Luther King, Jr., who didn't believe in violence. If you're on the other side of the fence, maybe one day you'll see the light and lead for all the right reasons. I've seen many gang leaders who were very charismatic people. Others followed them wherever they wanted them to go.

Real leadership can be a lonely road—look at the great leaders of the world and some of the tragedies they suffered. But sometimes you must be the voice of reason when everyone else seems to be going the wrong way. Being a leader means you have to stand up and say "no" when the group wants to hear something entirely different. Being a leader with integrity may not always make you very popular among your peers. Be different in the face of indifference—or even outright dissension.

HUMILITY AND RESPECT

I want to speak on humility because it is an important part of being a leader. Many of the world's great leaders are humble people. It's easy to think that we are special; little children think that way and big children do also. We *are* special but we don't have to be full of ourselves. We can be thankful and walk with our heads high, yet we can also be humble. Humility and greatness go hand in hand. We must humble ourselves in order to learn enough to be great.

Kevin Garnett's mother once told me something that really proved this point. Kevin was the talented, superstar basketball player for the Minnesota Timberwolves and was one of the most exciting players in the NBA. He was also one of the most gracious young people that's played the game. He came out of high school and went straight into the pros. I think his background is one of the reasons he adjusted so well. His mother told me that she had always shared with Kevin something that her own mother had told her long ago. She said, "The birds that fly the highest also have to come down to the ground to eat." I like that. No matter how big you become, that is one you can never forget. When I see a flock of geese I think of her words.

Phil Knight is a living example of this type of humility. The Knights are wonderful, regular people who have been really fortunate in their lives. But if you didn't know who they were, you would never suspect it. Phil may be a multibillionaire, but he still goes into the employee lunchroom every day and eats his lunch among his employees. That is the mark of true leaders. They stay accessible and open to their people so they can still learn from each other.

When we humble ourselves we open up the part of ourselves that can listen and learn. Humility also brings with it a sense of respect that can help us to avoid judging others. For example, it can sometimes be difficult to listen to older people. You may think that your parents have lost touch and just don't know what is happening in the world, because they are old and time has passed them by. I want to remind you that they have done or seen many of the things that you are thinking about doing; listen and learn from them. At the very least, they are traveling a road you will be going down yourself someday. Imagine how you'd like to be treated when you're in the same place. Your elders deserve your respect; make sure you give it to them and offer them a helping hand when they need it.

Everyone wants to be respected, but respect is one of those things that you have to give to get. You'll find out that as you give it, it will come back to you like clockwork. If you can't give any, don't expect any in return. And before you can give respect, and thus get it from others, you must first have respect for yourself.

On one of my trips, I started a conversation in the airport with a man named Mike Brown, who I learned was employed by Timex, the world-famous watchmakers. He had been with the company for nineteen years and was one of two blacks in the whole organization. I asked him about his experiences. He said, "I wouldn't have gotten this far if I hadn't met someone early on in my career who sat me down and gave me some good advice. When I first sat down with this person I felt like I was the biggest thing in the world. I was working for a big company and had a nice job. I really felt I was hot stuff. I had finally made it to the big leagues. Halfway through the process the gentleman stopped the interview and told me that he had a need to talk to me unofficially. He told me that if I kept the same attitude that I had I'd soon be out of a job." This stranger changed his life. Mike became more respectful and quite humble. He believed that the person who sat him down was responsible for where he is today.

On the other end of the scale, there's the guy who came up to me during a return visit to the University of Maryland. This man, who was homeless and penniless, was one of the same guys who had played ball with us. Not too long ago we'd all been on the same court together, and now he was on the street. He was one of the guys who didn't make it. Billy, the assistant coach, had put together a package of coats and gloves for him. This humbling experience really let me know how fine a line there is between making it and not making it. Just as the superstars are ordinary people at heart, so are the people who make the wrong turn. Nothing we have is permanent; it's important to remember that we come from, and go to, the same place in the end. Don't assume that what you have today you will have forever. Staying humble can help us truly value what we have, and being respectful of others can remind us that we all deserve respect.

AND-I MEDITATION

I respect myself and those around me, knowing that I can learn something from everyone I meet.

I am more humble now than I've ever been.

I feel my connection to the light in everything. It keeps me humble and gives me the strength to go out and accomplish great things.

SIXTEEN

Success

Do not seek to follow in the footsteps of the wise.
Seek what they sought.

—Basho

There is no specific recipe for success. Success may be as basic as raising a wonderful family. Or it may mean just being a happy, everyday person—not a sports star, or the smartest in your class, or a television or radio personality. It may be just that you go through life doing the right thing and teaching people by your example. You don't have to be someone known by the whole world in order to be successful. All you need to do is make a positive difference in your life and the lives of those around you.

Remember, do something that not everyone is willing to do. That's important. It might be as simple as getting up early to start your day. Think about it: there are only so many hours in a day—twenty-four of them, to be exact. Everyone gets the same twenty-four hours, every single day. Your goal is to better utilize your twenty-four; try to get more out of them. How you use your twenty-four hours is up to you. You can be as constructive with your time as you want to be—or as destructive.

123

Success doesn't depend on what other people think of what you're doing or what you've done. It's how you see it that counts. Start thinking of directions that you want your life to take. Maybe you want to follow in your parents' footsteps, or maybe you want a different life for yourself. You may not know exactly how to get there, but the thought process is the beginning. The next step will come to you.

You are not trying out anyone else's definition of success. The person who you must ultimately please is number one—and that is you. You should be the person who is hardest on your performance. Expect the most from yourself.

It's also important not to try to measure up to someone else, or feel bad because someone else does something better than you do. Actually, it's better that this happens, because if everyone did things the same way, what a boring world it would be! All you need to do is get those people who are better to help you become better at what you're doing. Don't be ashamed to ask them for help. They may be able to show you a better way. Likewise, if you have a special talent, don't be afraid to share it with someone else to help make that person better.

In truth, being successful simply means always doing things just a little bit better than you did before. You will be successful when you become your own best watchdog. Remember the formula: first, have a vision; second, write it down; third, decide what you'll sacrifice or give up to make it happen; and fourth, go about the business of making your vision come true. If you follow that procedure, I assure you that you will become a success.

AND-I EXECUTIVE

I didn't realize that I was an executive at Nike until I saw in the paper one day that the FBI was investigating "a high-level Nike executive." I wondered who was on the hot seat—little did I know that it was me! I didn't even know I'd reached executive status. For that matter, reaching executive status is still not something I particularly care about. I care that I provide a service and make things happen for Nike and my family.

It's what you do each and every day that makes you who you are. It's what people see you do as you go about the business of living your life. Live as who you are and make no excuses for the things you do. Always put your best foot forward and strive to do your best. It's not how you look or what you wear but who you are that can make a dif-ference. If people take this attitude and live by it, their value will far exceed that of any title. They will be an example, and that is the ultimate goal in any life: to lead and teach by example. Whether I'm an executive or just the next person you meet in a hallway, my example will always speak for me. Let yours speak for you.

125

BALANCE

Life is pretty basic and simple, but we complicate it with all the things that we think we want. Balance means being able to handle all of the things with which we are confronted, without neglecting any important part of ourselves. It's a continuous evolution.

I want to reiterate: life is quite simple. For every push there is a pull. Sometimes we have to pull back and look at the big picture so we can remember what we want to have happen in our lives.

It can be tough to do, but no matter what is going on around us it's always possible to stay in touch with our inner peace, our connection to ourselves and to all things. We seek peace within ourselves. We seek knowledge. We give and receive in equal measure.

Balance is the key to success and happiness. I once met a man who told me that because of where he grew up, he always had to fight to make it. Since he was always getting into fights, his mother put him in karate classes. He learned how to fight and protect himself, but he learned nothing more than that. He grew and matured, and then he met an instructor who told him that he'd learned enough about fighting—now he needed to learn who he was. This person said that he would enter a contest and would win until he reached the finals—but there he would always meet defeat. This new teacher taught him that competing should add balance to his life.

He began to feel the ebb and flow of life—the *yin* and *yang*. These things mean balance. In simple terms, everything has an equal. If there is an up, there must be a down. If there is a high, there must be a low. Nothing should ever be done in anger or frustration. There must always be an inner peace or balance. This comes from keeping your inner world free of extraneous thoughts. We are the ones who give permission for fear.

Since this man has embraced his new philosophy he has not lost a match. He has not approached his competition in anger. When they come at him with physical force, he uses mental force. When they go with mental, he comes with physical, but it is never in anger. This is a good lesson for all of us to learn. You have to know who you truly are to fully realize your goals.

FEAR

What is this thing we call fear? In its basic form it is just a feeling of doubt and insecurity. If you follow the path of this book, you will find that there is no need to have any sort of fear. You will see that it's an unnecessary barrier that gets in the way of your achieving the success that you deserve and want. I remember Michael Jordan saying that fear is an illusion. It is not real. We are the ones who give fear life by the way we think. Most of the things that we fear don't happen, and we spend a lot of time worrying about something that never happens.

127

In the Game of Life we can't afford to spend time worrying about what will or will not happen. If there is something that you can't control, don't spend a lot of time worrying about it. You need peace of mind and serenity. It doesn't hurt to have a little faith and to pray for your own strength; in the end, that inner strength will get you through the rough and painful times. Push the feeling of fear out of your mind and push forward. Forget those feelings of doubt. Let fear and insecurity leave by the same doors through which they entered. Replace worry and fear with self-confidence and faith.

You are the captain of your own ship, the master of your destiny. There is no true lack, no doubt, and no fear. These are all false feelings that are better replaced with feelings of truth and of confidence in yourself.

When I was in the eleventh grade I was invited to the Sid Fines All-American Basketball Camp in New York City. Coach Hathaway drove three of us to the camp that summer. This was New York; the Big Apple. When we got to the city, it was huge. The buildings were the biggest buildings I'd ever seen. They looked like they touched the sky. This was where the best basketball players in the world resided. This was it, I was here, in the place that I'd always heard about. This was the place where every basketball legend came from—New York, New York. Basketball had to have been born here in one of those huge buildings that touched the sky. I was just a little country boy from Hampton, Virginia. What was I doing in New York City?

It was scary to get on a crowded elevator or walk the streets with all of those people. Maybe my first visit here should have been a sightseeing tour, but I was here to play basketball. Even Coach Hathaway was scared. He was trying to persuade himself that everything would be fine, and that we were good players. We *were* good basketball players but the guys who lived in these huge buildings were the best in the world. I was scared to death! I didn't sleep that whole night before we had to play. I just lay there in a cold sweat thinking of the humble pie that we'd be eating. I remember leaving the hotel that morning. We looked at the people on the elevator with strange eyes—even causing someone on the elevator to ask us if something was wrong. What in the world were we doing here?

When we arrived at the gym and checked in, some of the other guys were already out there shooting around, and they didn't look like they were from another planet. They looked a little like me. So, the other guys and I went out and shot around with them. Boy, there were some big guys coming in to sign up. After a while someone shouted out, "Let's get a line going!" I didn't know what this was, so I just watched. They all got in a line and started shooting layups. Then they started dunking the ball all kinds of ways. This really was New York, and they were the best in the world! This was something to watch. It would have been good to be in the stands watching, but I was at the dance now and it was too late to go home. So, I had to go to work.

When we began to play, I was a little intimidated by where I had assessed my "game" against theirs. After a few times up and down the court, though, I started to feel like myself. I started to settle down and play the game. The place may have been bigger and some of the people different, but the court was the same as the one that I always played on. It became my world; I started to do the things that I always did. The fear factor left and the play factor became stronger and stronger. I dominated the play. They may not have known anything about Hampton when we came, but they knew about it when we left. I went home with the MVP trophy. When I left New York, I knew that all my fear had been for nothing. It was just an illusion. We usually get scared for no reason at all. Just face up to the task at hand and do your very best. Those guys were just guys. New York was just a place, and I left thinking that there wasn't a player from anywhere or at any height who was better than me.

The only thing that would and could beat me was me. From that day on, confidence was a way of life for me. I didn't always win, in sports or other things, but I always gave my best. Face every situation with supreme confidence. Remember, it is life's pleasure to grant you all the things that you desire and much more. There is only one person who can beat you, and that person is you.

AND-I MEDITATION

No matter what my situation, from this day forward I know that I will have all the things that I deserve. I know that they will come and I will work toward them in all that I do.

I define what makes me successful in life. I let my actions speak for me by fulfilling my responsibilities with dignity and energy. I recognize that fear is just an illusion, and I must consciously replace fearful thoughts with images of success.

I am more aware of all things around me and more alert to opportunities. With this new awareness I fear no more. I welcome adversity because it only serves to make me stronger. In any circumstance that confronts me, I see the good that it brings to me. I get from it the answers I need to make myself a better person.

SEVENTEEN

The Circle

★

There is nothing that is more complete than a circle. This is your cloak against the world. It is your protection, against doubt, against failure. The circle is complete; it has no beginning and it has no end. You are also complete. All you need, you have. So many of us think that we are missing something; you already have what you need, you simply need to find it.

Now, let's get back to the circle. Look at everything you do as a completed task. Whatever you do or attempt to do in your life, try to see it as already done. Envision in your mind's eye, in your imagination, a finished product. If you can see yourself starting something, also see yourself as finishing what you start. If you open something, close it. It just makes common sense. Why should you wait for someone else to come along and close what you've opened?

The circle is a big thing in my life. I see everything as complete. When it was basketball, I always saw the ball in the basket when I released it. I always saw it through the basket. If you study karate and you are breaking a board, you see the board as already broken before you hit it. You see *behind* the object that you are hitting. You don't just stop at the object but you see more; you see through the object. Everything that has ever happened started as an idea. If you believe in anything enough it will happen—either by your hands or the hands of someone else, but it will happen.

You can pick any spot in the circle as the beginning and you can pick any spot as the end. In life, if you can see a beginning, you must also see an end. You have to do your part and work toward that end but you won't be the determining factor. You may set the intention, but then you let go. You have to trust in something that is greater than yourself to make it happen when the time is right. Here we return to having faith and a positive outlook. Trust your own instincts and, more importantly, have faith in that force that connects all things.

Remember that the circle has no beginning and it has no end. Some lessons have to be learned over and over. Some you can learn once, and move on to the next. Don't rely on your gifts alone, but be sure to make the sacrifice and do the work to make things happen. By forming discipline and good habits, you give yourself a solid foundation from which anything is possible. See the task as complete and do everything in your power to make it happen.

If you have no foundation, you have nowhere to turn when things go awry. If you fly by the seat of your pants, how do you fly when you have no pants? This happens to a lot of good ballplayers. They all have natural talent but don't work on their game. When they're elevated to the next level, where everyone is good and has also worked hard to excel, those who haven't worked usually fall by the wayside. If it's easy, it might be great today, but I'll tell you—and I hope you listen to this—one day you'll be starting over again. Do you want your foundation to be weak or strong?

The same is true of those great students who don't learn to study. They might get good grades in high school, but when they go to college they find that the work is harder and they have very bad study habits. Consequently, their grades aren't that great and they don't really know how to change it all around. Then they have to start all over again and learn the proper way to study in order to stay in school. The circle is continuous.

COUNT YOUR BLESSINGS

Someone once said, "Let gratitude be your attitude."

This is a simple process. We should give thanks for all the things that come to us each and every day. We take so many things for granted. Give thanks for waking up each day, for the food you eat, and for all the good things that happen to you. It's a good habit to form. The more you do this, the less you will take anything for granted. Nothing is just "supposed" to be the way it is. Let that be the first thought that comes to your mind each morning. It didn't happen because there was no other way for things to turn out—it definitely doesn't *have* to be this way. This understanding shifts the focus more to the giving mode than the taking mode. Those with this awareness tend to be much more humble. People get so hung up on all the material things they think they need. They want and want and take for granted that they can walk around, that they can see, that they are alive. Just count your blessings, both big and small, each and every day. If you focus on all the things that you have—a warm bed to sleep in, food to eat, friends and family to love—it will remind you of what is truly important. For you are greatly blessed.

I discussed the manuscript for this book with a woman who told me she had been reading more positive books, and they had made all the difference in her life. She used to think her beauty was in the makeup she wore or how her hair was styled. She told me that now the way she looked was the way she felt. Before, little things could wreck her entire day. The way people treated her could affect her outlook, as well as her self-image. Now, she gets up in the morning and gives thanks for the day. She rolls back the curtains and listens for a bird singing or feels the sun on her face. She gives thanks, whatever the weather. She smells the beauty of life and this starts her day. From there, nothing that people do can make any impact on her outlook on life. She enjoys wonderful conversations with many people and they make her feel special. She is now in control of her own mood and, ultimately, her destiny.

GIVING BACK

Ralph Waldo Emerson said, "The only gift is a portion of thyself." The best way to give thanks is to share what you've gotten, to give it back to others. I've run across several people of late who have let me know that writing this book was the right thing to do. They told me of the difficulties of life before they came into the light of understanding and love. They told me how, with limited knowledge and confidence, they struggled to make decisions and just weren't sure of themselves. I'm happy to share what I've learned to help others overcome those obstacles, just as so many people have helped me. The circle continues. We give and we receive. We keep the cycle going.

The most important thing about giving to others is that you can never know what impact on the world your help may have. When you look at a child, you can't see whether the cure for cancer is locked away inside him or her—but if it is, it may never come out without encouragement. People have enormous potential that we can't know until their gifts have been unlocked, until they've seen their visions for their own futures. Some people may be able to do it on their own, **135** but most of us need a helping hand. Sometimes all people need is to realize that other people care about what happens to them. That inspires them to work harder, because they want those other people to be proud of them. There are a lot of distractions out there that make life hard and make dreams seem impossible. Do what you can to light the path for others.

MY CIRCLE OF MENTORS

It's funny, but a lot of the people who come into my life come into it for a reason. That is what keeps me positive and keeps me moving forward. Phil Knight became one of my mentors and has led me along the path of business. If we go back to the circle, Phil coming into my professional life was the same as Coach Hathaway coming in when I first started to play basketball. Phil directs me in making decisions that are extremely important in my life. Phil has been in my corner ever since we met. I don't know why the relationship between my family and the Knights became special; I think it was something that the forces of the universe just put together. It was the same with Coach Hathaway and Barbara. Barbara is Coach Hathaway's wife, and she was like a mother to me. She cared for me just like I was one of hers. I remember when college coaches would come to see me play, she would give them the third degree. She would talk to them about education and what the school had to offer me as a student athlete. Half the time I didn't know what she was talking about. She was on her

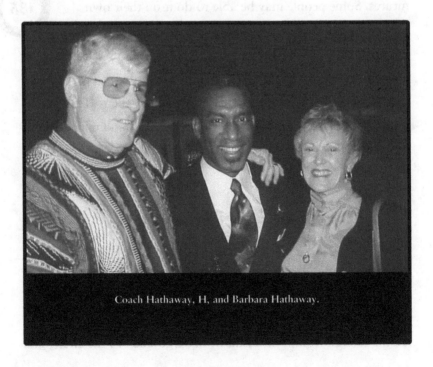

Coach Hathaway, H, and Barbara Hathaway.

own path, but it turned out to be great for me. The Hathaways were and still are to this day just caring people.

Now, just as Coach Hathaway took me aside and told me that I could be just like the "Big O," Phil took me aside one day when we were in his inner office. We were talking about the future; my question to him was, How far could I go in the company? He pointed to his chair and said I could get all the way to that seat. That made me smile on the inside (and on the outside too, I think). I don't know how far I will go at Nike, but I like the way that he thinks. That type of confidence is something that inspires people to great heights. In the business world, Phil has been the same as Coach Hathaway was in the world of sports and basketball. He has given me a picture to lock onto and see; he has given me a vision. Sometimes eyes cannot see and ears cannot hear. That just happens to be most people. Don't let that be you. Listen to those people who come into your life to help you.

Whether my dream happens exactly as I had expected is not important. Where I end up is not up to me, but rather up to the infinite intelligence. What is up to me is to work my hardest and make the best out of what I have before me. This allows me to experience other unforeseen opportunities as they arise. Remember the incident of my being investigated by the FBI? Penny Knight fought for me just as Barbara Hathaway had fought for me. Penny wanted me to fight back. I didn't know who to fight. I have no fear in these matters, because I know that if one door closes it only means that a bigger one will open up. Just have faith and be trusting and the right thing will happen.

137

Our faith must be tested. How else will we know how truly strong we are or need to be?

Now, I'm not saying that you should read this book and go right out and stare your enemy down and feel that he can't hurt you. Sadly, we've entered a time when people shoot people for looking at them the wrong way. The fact is, this is something that takes time. You have to work on developing this faith and trust in the ways of the world and know that you are a part of all things and all things are a part of you. If you have the most powerful force in the universe on your side, whom will you fear? The trick to this is *always knowing* this force is there. Oftentimes we don't believe it, because this is something we can't see in the physical world. Or because something bad happens and we don't see how things will ever be good again. But it is there. Always there!

RULE NO. 1 AND RULE NO. 101

The most important rule in life is the simplest thing in the world. It is the first rule that we learned in school. They still teach it; we just seem to forget it all too easily. Rule number 1 and rule number 101 is the golden rule. This does *not* mean "he who has the gold rules." The real meaning and the one that will do you the most good is: "Do unto others as you would have them do unto you."

I once asked a good friend of mine, who happens to be the CEO of a Fortune 500 company, to what he owed his success. He felt that what he did was treat people the way he himself wanted to be treated. I saw him going around his office addressing each of the employees by their first name. This was quite impressive. He got it! He treated them the way he wanted to be treated. Here is the power of the circle once again. You get back what you put out. You get what you give.

I am you, you are me, we are one. And together we can make this a better world.

If I can be the vice president of the number-one sports and fitness apparel company in the world, you can be anything you desire.

We all have tough times, but that is what really makes life worth living. This summer my life flashed before my eyes. I kept having shortness of breath and it got worse and worse. At first I thought I was just in horrible shape since I'd recently had a hip replacement. In the end I got so bad my wife ended up rushing me to the ER and they admitted me into the hospital. I was later diagnosed with congestive heart failure.

I was as healthy as I thought anyone could be. I ate good, exercised regularly. I wasn't a drinker and I never smoked. This diagnosis didn't seem to add up, but it also taught me that there are no guarantees in life! One day all is well and the next second things can all change. Like what Beyoncé sings about in one of her songs: I went to bed on top of the world and woke up with the world on top of me.

After undergoing numerous tests and sending samples to the Mayo Clinic, my doctor visited me in my hospital room one afternoon and explained that though they didn't have all the results quite yet, I may end up needing a heart transplant. "I know this isn't the news you want to hear," he said "but I just want to prepare you for the worst." It was very hard news but there are things in life that are difficult. As we spoke I got over the initial shock and started to ask questions in order to prepare for the road ahead. What has gotten me where I am in life is my faith and belief.

I was prepared for whatever we had to do and I told my doctor that I am putting my faith in him, and that God will bring me through this journey. The doctor left, but only a short while later, he returned, closing the door behind him. He looked at Donna and me and said, "I've never seen anyone with this amount of faith. It is truly inspiring."

This book is a testimony to how I have chosen to live my life. Oh, and by the way, the results did finally come back. I didn't need a heart transplant. They felt they could control my complications with medicines. Believe to Achieve, See the Invisible, and Do the Impossible. I hope you're able to overcome all of your adversity in life.

As you travel through life the circle will be your protection. Your apprenticeship may be difficult at times. You will have many trials and tribulations. But these moments will define your true character. Only through these trials can you achieve your ultimate goal. Your fate will be in your hands and you will be the master of your destiny. You will recognize your choices and make right decisions. You will have confidence in all you do. When you come full circle—you then have the responsibility and obligation to lead those who follow. Through perseverance and faith, you will achieve the ultimate goal of becoming an And-I Master.

The And-I.

Thee and I.

AND-I MEDITATION

And-I . . . am.

. . . I am a source of power and positive thought in this world.

I am for all things that are right and wonderful.

This new magnificent power flows through me and makes me whole.

It gives me all that I need to make things happen.

I am full of life.

Each of my cells is filled with light.

I no longer "do" great things but great things happen through me, for I am already a part of them.

I do my best when I am still and in tune with my inner self. When I know this inner thought, I know who I am.

I see myself as a wonder of the universe. I am now a part of all things and all things are a part of me. I am a being of strength and direction who is focused and I have my eye on the sparrow.

I keep my temper at all times because I am in control of myself. I have the courage and strength to walk away from any disagreeable situation. If I must stand, I do so in truth and honesty and with renewed power and strength.

When I meet people, I realize they have come into my life for a reason. I'm open to what they offer for me to learn and I look forward to learning new and exciting things.

I am a resource of learning for others and will teach what I know to those who want to hear.

Just as an eagle can see a fish, swoop down, and catch it while barely touching the water, I realize that I can do many things, for I have this same perfection in me.

I am a special creation of the universe. I am unique. I will never again think that I am something less than I really am. And I am an And-I.

The circle is complete.

The Goal

I use my Mind
> For it is my weapon against fear.

I use my Shield of Faith
> For it is my protection.

I go into the world
> To change it a little for the better each day.

Right after I make up my bed.

I am an And-I warrior.

(Signature: "H. White") _____

                              name

The Impact
and Future of
Believe to Achieve

Believe to Achieve has been given countless times as gifts for family and friends over the past 15 years. It's even been given to people in prison. I've always been truly humbled when I hear about their stories and the actions my book has inspired.

One such story was about a woman from Chicago who was struggling day-to-day. So, she had visited her local library with the intention of getting a book that could help motivate her. She ended up not finding the book she had intended to checkout, but she did find *Believe to Achieve* and decided to check it out and give it a try. She started reading the book that day on the bus ride home and she didn't stop until she finished it. She was so engrossed that she almost missed her stop. She later wrote to tell me that the book was just what the doctor ordered.

Another of my favorite inspiring stories was about a little girl who had visited the Nike offices with the Make-A-Wish Foundation. I got to meet her and she surprised me by telling me that she'd read *The Power of Hello* and how it had changed her life. (*The Power of Hello* was a NPR radio interview I did, which they chose to transcribe and include as the first essay in the NPR book *This I Believe*, a collection of their most popular interviews on the subject of "belief.") This young girl was so inspired by my words that she went on to write a paper for school that she titled the "Power of Positivity." And the best part of her story was that during all these chance events—reading my interview to writing her paper—she was empowered to the point where the process helped her get through stage 4 brain cancer. She's one of my heroes.

I had always been very satisfied with the impact the book was having out in the world. All the shared stories were just amazing. But then I heard about two people who were having an entirely new experience with it—new successes that blew my expectations for what *Believe to Achieve* could do for others.

There was Malcolm Teasdale, a high school principal in Detroit, who started using the book as a tool to help students with disciplinary problems at his school. Malcolm noticed how those students who had read *Believe to Achieve* started to show changes in behavior as well as an entirely new outlook on school. Students started getting better grades and other teachers started asking their peers (who were using the book in class) how this was happening. Soon after, other schools—public and charter schools—started to take notice of the positive changes the kids were undergoing and started asking questions and wanting to implement the book into their schools.

To help focus and facilitate the teachings from the book, Malcolm created his own lesson guide for parents, teachers, and mentors so that *Believe to Achieve* could be used as a tool in schools and communities by anyone who was interested. Malcolm told me that there was a growth of popularity with people throughout his community who were eagerly using the book as a practical mentoring program and that the concepts in the book were reaching even more people. To top it all off, they were also now using Malcolm's guide along with the book as they implemented the teachings into their daily work. I couldn't have asked for more. The book had taken on a life of its own and the impact was spreading.

And then there was Michelle Martin, a community activist and mentoring expert in Philadelphia, who started using *Believe to Achieve* in community groups like Philadelphia Fire Explorers and Youth Service Inc., another community group that services homeless and runaway youth. Michelle used the book as a tool to motivate, to help guide others through daily challenges, and ulti-mately help people take charge in changing their own lives. Michelle and her husband Anthony, who own the nonprofit Urban Youth Racing School, gave thousands of books away at their "What it Takes" events, which are mentoring seminars infused with e-mentoring (aka guided mentoring using online technology) that give youth a firsthand experience about what it takes to be successful.

In 2014, Malcolm and Michelle contacted me. They had discussed the success they had both witnessed when Malcolm's lesson guide was used along with *Believe to Achieve* when teach-ing students. They felt it was their duty to contact me to share their success stories and to urge me to include the guide as a tool within the book so that anyone who was interested could have a fuller experience. It was music to my ears!

In this updated edition of *Believe to Achieve* you'll find just that: Malcolm's tried and tested Parent, Teacher, and Mentor Lesson Guide. Everyone can fly with a little help and this guide is just the tool to help anyone soar if they so choose.

If you or your group needs help to implement the teachings in this book and lesson guide, please do not hesitate to reach out to us. And if you want to share your success stories, I'd love to hear those too. Visit www.HowardHWhite.com to share your tale.

Parent, Teacher, and Mentor Lesson Guide

This lesson guide was designed to draw a direct connection between the reader and their immediate support system in life. Parents, teachers, and mentors are a student's lifeline.

All lessons presented in the guide consist of objectives, activities, and assessments geared towards reinforcing the many lessons and illustrations taught and described by Howard "H" White. The author's commitment to the reader's is to entertain, inform, and spark a sense of motivation in the reader and this lesson guide's purpose is to assist the facilitator in presenting the pathway for each reader to find their gift as well as "the inner me."

The Mirror

Not just a dreamer who hopes to achieve,
In order to do that, I had to BELIEVE.

OBJECTIVE:

Introduce the idea of visualizing a positive outcome.

PROCESS:

1. Read "The Mirror" poem on page xix (as a class).
2. Highlight all positive thoughts or words described in the poem.
3. Student driven: select the phrase or line that best describes you or your life at the present time.

ACCOUNTABLE TALK SEGMENT:

As a group discuss the poem's purpose and value:

- Define each positive thought or phrase.

- Encourage students to talk about what phrases relate to them.

TEACHABLE MOMENT:

Watch Howard "H" White's live reading of his poem "The Mirror" at www.HowardHWhite.com to introduce the concept of driving the point with the driving question.

ASSESSMENT:

Students will write a brief response to the driving question (below) and post it on the front of their assigned folder, journal, or notebook. This response will be revisited throughout the reading of *Believe to Achieve*.

Driving Question: What is your hoop in life?

LESSON 1

Vision (Chapter 1)

*You need an image in your mind that you can
hold up and work toward.*

OBJECTIVE:

Write a brief description of what you would like to accomplish
over the next five years.

PROCESS:

1. List all of your strengths and weaknesses.
2. List at least three distractions that may interrupt your progress over the next five years.
3. Pair and share your thoughts with a peer.
4. View H's "Vision" and "Hardwork" videos at www.HowardHWhite.com.

ACCOUNTABLE TALK SEGMENT:

- As a group discuss solutions for eliminating or limiting distractions.

- Each student should share at least three distractions.

- Revisit the phrase: "You're a part of the problem or a part of the solution."

- For each distraction listed there should be a solution or an idea that suggests a solution that is possible and worth exploring.

TEACHABLE MOMENT:

All students must leave the first session with a sense of accomplishment. Compliments and encouraging words are recommended. For example: Mentioning and discussing well organized thoughts, writing, and interesting goals for the five-year plan.

ASSESSMENT:

Ask students to complete this statement: *Being a part of the solution means as a young person I must continue or begin to do the following.* (Note: Have students list their solutions).

LESSON 2

Goal Setting (Chapter 2)

Have a clear vision.

OBJECTIVE:

- Review chapter 1 and the "Vision" exercise.

- Introduce the Believe to Achieve pillars of success.

PROCESS:

Define and describe the following terms to all students:

1. Visualize

2. Write it down

3. Sacrifice

4. Do the work

5. Always know

(Note: These interpretations are at the discretion of the facilitator combined with H's point of view from the book.)

ACCOUNTABLE TALK SEGMENT:

In two-minute intervals the facilitator will ask each student to recite the pillars of success with a brief description.

TEACHABLE MOMENT:

- All students should leave the second session with a sense of accomplishment. Compliments and encouraging words are highly recommended.

- Ask each student to announce which portion of the lesson they enjoyed the most. (Note: At this point you're asking students to find something to look forward to for the next session.)

CREATING A VISION BOARD:

Materials needed: Magazines, paper, scissors, and glue.

1. Find a quiet time when you can reflect. Think about what you have learned in chapter 1 and 2 of the book.

2. Ponder. Analyze your different roles and parts of your life that are important to you and write them out so you can see them.

3. Dream. Close your eyes and go through each category and visualize what your ideal would be in each category. What does that look like for you? What does it feel like? What does it smell like? What does it sound like? What does it taste like? Then write down words that come to mind in describing each category.

4. Set your intention. Now that you have identified the areas of your life: choose one to five areas that you want to focus on for the year and intentionally be working on. Now, decide if you want to do one large board with all of the areas, or if you want to divide them into individual categories.

157

5. Find images that speak to you. Browse through magazines and find images that speak to you. Get out of your head and just go with what your heart tells you. What this means is for you to not specifically go looking for images or words, but instead let those images find you. It doesn't have to be literally what you are hoping to achieve but may embody a feeling instead. Then when you feel like you have enough images you are ready to get them on paper.

6. Begin to place the images on the page. Start placing the larger images in the back without any real set plan on how it will look.

7. Glue it on the paper. Place them as you see fit. Be as creative as you can.

8. Set an action item for each category. Taking an additional step in writing verbal action items can help give you a place to begin. For each category write down one to three goals, and make them specific and clear.

9. Hang it where you can see it and revisit it often. Visit it every three to six months to see where you are with your goals. It is a good idea to do a new board once a year.

(Note: As you reach some of your goals and your life changes you should make those adjustments.)

ASSESSMENT:

Students should list at least five goals over the next five years and describe how the five pillars will assist them in accomplishing their goals.

Make It Happen
(Chapter 3)

Think about the steps you can take everyday to
move closer to your goal.

OBJECTIVE:

- Review *Believe to Achieve* vision board.

- Introduce the concept of sacrificing early in life and how to defer the gratification process.

PROCESS:

1. Read your communication to a peer or a group of peers.
2. Explain why you chose the particular profession or the professional.

ACCOUNTABLE TALK SEGMENT:

Good things come to those who wait and exercise patience:

- Students will individually create a list of things that are worth sacrificing.

- Pair students in groups of three to discuss and record their selections on a chart.

- As a class construct a list of items worth sacrificing.

TEACHABLE MOMENT:

- Define the terminology: "Delayed Gratification."

- Reinforce the lesson with reference to H's video "Sacrifice:" that can be found at www.Howardhwhite.com.

ASSESSMENT:

Ask students to complete the following task (due next session):

1. Explain why sacrifice is necessary.
2. Describe the connection between sacrifice and delayed gratification.

(Note: If time permits plan one on one time with students to review their thoughts about the day's lesson.)

LESSON 4

Best Foot Forward
(Chapter 4)

Look for situations that can
give you an edge.

OBJECTIVE:

- Review *Believe to Achieve* vision board.

- "Pennies are positive thoughts:" Penny in the jar concept and theory. (Note: At the conclusion of the lesson students will be able to define the formula for success.)

- Formula for Success: Habit + Discipline + Structure = Success

PROCESS:

1. Provide a penny jar for the class to contribute to each day or class session.

2. Materials: Jars, water, pennies, replica pennies or notes to place in jar. (Note: This is at the facilitator's discretion.)

ACCOUNTABLE TALK SEGMENT:

• Group discussion on the Formula for Success: define the terms as a class and discuss the importance of each.

• Relate this to filling up a penny jar...pennies equal positive thoughts.

• Describe and discuss the displacement of the water.

TEACHABLE MOMENT:

• How is habit created?

• How to create structure?

• How does discipline lead to success?

ASSESSMENT:

All students will prepare a graphic organizer displaying the Formula for Success. This can be described based on the student(s) imagination and self-perception. (Note: The organizer can also display as a list, semantic map, and/or chart.)

Responsibility (Chapter 5)

You can be part of the problem or
you can be part of the solution.

OBJECTIVE:

- Review *Believe to Achieve* vision board.

- Read and discuss the lesson "H" learned regarding "responsibility." By the end of the lesson students will demonstrate the ability to recognize the value in responsibility, and the advantages and disadvantages when responsibility is not exercised in a positive manner.

- View H's "Life Lessons" video at www.HowardHWhite.com.

PROCESS:

1. A group discussion about responsibility and its characteristics. (Note: Groups will consist of two or three students)
2. The groups will create a role-play situation in which responsibility is utilized in a positive manner.
3. Facilitator summarizes and comments on the group presentations.

ACCOUNTABLE TALK SEGMENT:

Facilitator will review the lesson "H" learned and relate it to the group presentations.

TEACHABLE MOMENT:

Accountability: "Accept your shortcomings and improve on them." Discuss the meaning of this statement. (For example: Encourage students to define accountability and link the definition to responsibility.)

ASSESSMENT:

In a brief summary describe why "H" lost his privilege to carry a patrol belt. Reinforce the definition of accountability and responsibility.

Change (Chapter 6)

*Even if something doesn't go the way you
want it to, look for the hidden gift.*

OBJECTIVE:

- Have your students review their *Believe to Achieve* vision board.

- Create a list of characteristics describing how "change" occurs.

PROCESS:

1. Divide students into groups of five.
2. Ask students to list characteristics of "change."

3. Groups will present the characteristics to the class as a whole.

ACCOUNTABLE TALK SEGMENT:

- A class discussion: Students will talk about examples of people in society that have demonstrated change. Examples may include: famous people, family members, friends, and others.

- What do the people discussed have in common?

- Did their commitment to change truly benefit them?

TEACHABLE MOMENT:

Define the statement: "If there's one certainty in life, it is that everything must change." (Note: Encourage students to hold themselves accountable and reflect on their actions.)

STUDENT SKILL DEVELOPMENT:

Recall, reflect, and write. (Note: These reinforcement skills may also serve as discussion points to engage prior knowledge at the beginning of the remaining sessions.)

ASSESSMENT:

Ask students to list three things as students they would like to change about themselves.

Mentors (Chapter 7)

*Try to look for positive people so their
influence is both positive and uplifting.*

OBJECTIVE:

- Have your students review their *Believe to Achieve* vision board.

- To define and identify the role of a mentor and a mentee's responsibility; by completing this lesson the student should be able to define the role of both mentor and mentee.

Process:

1. On an index card ask students to select a person in their life that they would consider to be trustworthy, kind, respectful, and great to know.
2. On the back of the same index card ask students to list that person's greatest attributes or qualities.

Accountable Talk Segment:

As a group or class create a "Mentor's Checklist" in which all students contribute at least two or three attributes from their index cards.

Teachable Moment:

Being able to select the right person to serve as mentor requires several characteristics.

Assessment:

Students must articulate the following responses in two forms—written and verbal.

Students must also demonstrate the ability to read/analyze people and recognize the "good" in people.

LESSON 7.2

Mentors (Chapter 7)

Try to look for positive people so their
influence is both positive and uplifting.

OBJECTIVE:

- Have your students review their *Believe to Achieve* vision board.

- Lesson review: To define and identify the role of a mentor and a mentee's responsibility; by completing this lesson the student should be able to define the role of both mentor and mentee.

REVISIT THE TEACHABLE MOMENT:

Being able to select the right person to serve as a mentor requires several characteristics.

PROCESS:

1. On an index card ask students to list what they feel a mentor would look for in them.
2. On the back of the same index card ask students to write their greatest attributes or qualities.

ACCOUNTABLE TALK SEGMENT:

As a group or class create a "Mentee's Checklist" in which all students contribute at least two or three attributes from their index cards.

TEACHABLE MOMENT:

Being the best person YOU can be will serve as a great connection to gaining a great mentor.

ASSESSMENT:

An important skill for a student is to create a positive represen-
tation in an effort to attract a mentor that works for them. Your
students should practice articulating the following responses in
two forms—written and verbal:

- Where would you expect to find a positive mentor?

- How do you plan on building a connection to them?

173

Rules of the Game
(Chapter 8)

Rules give everyone the chance to be someone.
People can learn the rules and then work on
improving their game.

OBJECTIVE:

• Review *Believe to Achieve* vision board.

• Understand and grasp the concept of Discipline and the Rules of Life.

PROCESS:

1. Revisit the story of the two dogs (page 43).
2. Divide the class or group in half.
3. Ask each group to represent one of the dogs.

4. Both groups will list the characteristics of the dog they represent.

5. Facilitator will present the outcome of each dog.

ACCOUNTABLE TALK SEGMENT:

Part 1

- Class discussion in which students will compare and contrast both dogs and decide which dog had the most success and why.

- Student will be required to explain the following:

  o What role did discipline play in the outcome of the dogs?

  o What could they learn from both dogs?

Part 2

- The concept and theory of Knowing the Rules.

- How does knowing the Rules of the Game apply to me?

ASSESSMENT:

Create a set of five rules to follow for the remainder of the year. (Note: Revisit the individual rules at the opening of the next session.)

LESSON 9

Strength (Chapter 9)

There are moments that test us all.
Not everything in life is simple.

OBJECTIVE:

- Review *Believe to Achieve* vision board.

- Define strength and provide scenarios in which strength prevailed.

PROCESS:

1. Pair and share exercise.
2. Pair students and ask them to share a situation in which their strength was tested. All pairs must record the scenarios and be prepared to share with the group.

(Note: The purpose of this exercise is to share the realization that all people are tested and how we respond is the most important factor.)

ACCOUNTABLE TALK SEGMENT:

- What defines strength or being strong?

- How do we distinguish mental strength from physical strength?

TEACHABLE MOMENT:

Reference the term "in spite of" and discuss the theory behind H's term.

ASSESSMENT:

Persistence and strength will equal a positive outcome for your students. Have them complete the following sentence: *In spite of (insert challenge/hardship), strength and belief in myself helped me win the battle.*

Believe (Chapter 10)

Listen to yourself and do what's best for you.

OBJECTIVE:

- Review *Believe to Achieve* vision board.

- Recognize the dream and see it clearly.

- Believe in yourself through high self-esteem and growing confidence.

PROCESS:

1. Refer to the second chapter on vision.
2. Revisit the original exercise.

3. Vision Terminology:

> Visualize
>
> Write it Down
>
> Sacrifice
>
> Do the Work
>
> Always Know

4. Create a graphic organizer with your "dream" serving as the main reference (see below).

ACCOUNTABLE TALK SEGMENT:

- Group discussion on a person's "self-esteem" and how it pays to have "self-esteem."

- Discuss the concept of building confidence.

- Define resilient.

TEACHABLE MOMENT:

Review the "in spite of" theme; draw a connection between the previous theme and building "self-esteem."

ASSESSMENT:

Write a brief summary of the concepts covered:

- See the dream

- Utilize the vision (focus)

- Grow your confidence

- Build your self-esteem

(Note: Ask students: How, When, What, Where, and Why)

GRAPHIC ORGANIZER TEMPLATE

Power (Chapter 11)

It is the power that makes all things happen,
and the connection to it is what separates the
weak from the strong.

OBJECTIVE:

- To teach and encourage students to develop an atmosphere in which they can define the power of the mind and strong thoughts.

- Introduce the term "reflection" and the manner in which reflection can serve as an act of support for thinking clearly and positively.

DRIVING QUESTION:

How can a strong mind and strong thoughts lead to the truth within your life?

GROUP DISCUSSION:

Building a strong mindset and creating strong thoughts are essential for finding the truth in your life.
Discussion points may include the following:

- Positive versus negative thoughts.

- Good intentions versus not so good intentions.

- Creating positive outcomes when challenged with negative obstacles.

ACTIVITY:

At the conclusion of the lesson students will demonstrate the ability to create a "Map to the Zone of Truth."

PROCESS:

1. List all of the things in your life that are negative or not so good.

2. List all of the positive things in your life or the great things.

3. Describe which things you see in your future.

4. Visualize yourself five years from now.

ASSESSMENT:

On clear white paper or on an iPad etc. sketch the vision of yourself five years from now.

Include your profession, family, friends, etc.

LESSON 12

Spirit (Chapter 12)

When one door closes, another opens,
and you must always have faith in that.

OBJECTIVE:

- Establish a method to searching the human spirit for the right answers.

- Make a life connection to the philosophy of "faith."

DRIVING QUESTION:

How do we develop inner strength and peace?

ACTIVITY:

Visualization: Have students close their eyes and create a center of focus and picture themselves as adults in their desired profession. After five minutes ask all students to demonstrate verbally what they pictured. (Facilitator will document the responses on chart or grid paper.)

GROUP DISCUSSION:

Guided Questions:

1. How can we connect "faith" to developing an "inner strength" and "peace?"
2. How can faith, inner strength, and peace play a role in accomplishing your desired goals?
3. Does the human spirit need all of the discussed characteristics in order to be effective?

ASSESSMENT:

- At the conclusion of the lesson students will demonstrate the ability to draw a connection between faith, inner strength, peace, and the human spirit.

- Physical Description Exercise: Create an "Open and Close Door" list (this may be referenced as a "cause and effect" chart).

  o List all the times you were excited or planned something.

  o Add the obstacle that may have stopped your plan or ended your excitement.

  o List the alternative plan you would use to move around the obstacle.

  o Add your plan in moving forward beyond the obstacles.

Love (Chapter 13)

In everything you see, focus on the good.
Learn to love the smaller thing.

OBJECTIVE:

Introduce the concepts of friends, happiness, and forgiveness. At the conclusion of the lesson and activities, students will demonstrate the ability to distinguish the concepts of friends, happiness, and forgiveness.

DRIVING QUESTION:

What connection can you make between friends, happiness, forgiveness, and love?

ACTIVITY:

- Pair and share—Friendship Interview

- Students form a pair and ask each other the following questions:

  o How have you made friends?

  o Who do you consider a friend?

  o How do make or find good friends?

  o What role can "love" play in this process?

GROUP DISCUSSION:

1. Was there a time when you had to forgive someone?
2. Was there a time when you had to ask for forgiveness?
3. How does forgiving someone make you a stronger person?
4. What role does "love" play in forgiveness?

ASSESSMENT:

Draw and create a picture of "love." Begin with a mental view and translate the mental version onto paper or iPad etc. You may include the symbols of friendship, forgiveness, and happiness.

LESSON 14

Passion (Chapter 14)

Get excited about life and go for it with
all your heart and soul.

OBJECTIVE:

Students will complete the session with a personal interpretation of "passion" and how it is present in their life.

DRIVING QUESTION:

As young people how can you find your "passion" in life? How can you find what you're truly passionate about?

ACTIVITY:

Students will translate the following sayings as quoted by H:

1. Do things with "passion."
2. Seek people who have already done what you aspire to do or be?
3. Put your best foot forward.

(Note: All responses will be presented during group discussion segment.)

GROUP DISCUSSION:

Translations will be discussed in a group of five students.

OBJECTIVE TWO:

Students will demonstrate the ability to draw a direct connection between "passion" and finding their "gift" thus far in life:

1. Define the concept of a "gift."
2. Discuss as a class.
3. Students will write their "gifts" on colored index cards.

ASSESSMENT:

On a poster large board post all index card responses from students. (Note: The poster board should be displayed as a collage.)

LESSON 15

Honor (Chapter 15)

*Get excited about life and go for it with
all your heart and soul.*

197

OBJECTIVE:

Students will complete the session with a personal interpretation of "honor" and how it is present in their life.

ACTIVITY ONE:

Students will translate the following sayings as quoted by H:

1. "Honor is something that no amount of fame and fortune can buy."
2. "Keep confidence and integrity, and you will always have a solid and firm ground on which to stand tall."

OBJECTIVE TWO:

Students will demonstrate the ability to define honesty, leadership, humility, and respect.

ACTIVITY TWO:

Students will translate the following sayings as quoted by H:

1. "Humility and greatness go hand in hand."
2. "When you are dishonest with yourself the only one that loses is you."
3. "Real leadership can be a lonely road."

ACCOUNTABLE TALK:

Students will form interview questions for facilitator based on the key definitions discussed.

STUDENT ASSESSMENT:

All students will write a 250-word "Honor" essay describing how they plan on incorporating the following key terms into their life in moving forward:

- Honor

- Humility and Respect

- Leadership

- Honesty

Assignment to be submitted and read shared aloud during the opening of the next session.

LESSON 16

Success (Chapter 16)

*All you have to do is make a positive difference
in your life and the lives around you.*

PRESENT "HONOR" ESSAYS

Students will do an oral presentation of their essay to the class.

OBJECTIVE:

Students will describe what "success" means to them.

ASSESSMENT:

Students to create a written reflection on the meaning of success.
Assessment Guidelines:

- The inner and outer handbook lessons may be used as references.

- Students are encouraged to revisit all previous lessons, created materials, and projects.

- The reflection should include responses to the following guided questions:

  o How do you define success?

  o Why is success important?

  o How have you prepared to achieve success?

- The short reflection should be completed and submitted by the end of the session.

WRITTEN REFLECTION RUBRIC:

1. Proper grammar
2. Clear thoughts
3. Include definitions and explanations
4. Use examples
5. Proper sentence structure
6. Legible handwriting/penmanship

The Circle
(Chapter 17)

*There is nothing that is more complete
than a circle.*

*If you can see yourself starting something, also
see yourself as finishing what you start.*

OBJECTIVE:

All participants completing the program will demonstrate mastery of all lessons by creating a "Circle" of truth and values. The circle will display all components presented and learned from these lessons. The center of the circle should display the student's GOAL(s) in life.